Francis S Smith

Poems for the Million

Francis S Smith
Poems for the Million
ISBN/EAN: 9783744710602
Printed in Europe, USA, Canada, Australia, Japan
Cover: Foto ©Thomas Meinert / pixelio.de

More available books at **www.hansebooks.com**

POEMS FOR THE MILLION.

BY

Francis S. Smith.

WRITTEN FOR AND PUBLISHED FROM TIME TO TIME IN THE COLUMNS OF STREET & SMITH'S "NEW-YORK WEEKLY."

NEW-YORK:

PUBLISHED FOR THE AUTHOR BY THE AMERICAN NEWS COMPANY.

1871.

Entered, according to Act of Congress, in the year 1871, by
FRANCIS S. SMITH,
in the Office of the Librarian of Congress, at Washington.

TO THE PATRONS OF

STREET & SMITH'S NEW-YORK WEEKLY,

WHOSE KIND APPRECIATION HAS ENCOURAGED ME TO HOPE THAT MY

EFFORTS IN THE FIELD OF POESY MIGHT BE RECEIVED BY THE

GENERAL PUBLIC WITH SOME LITTLE FAVOR,

THIS VOLUME OF

"POEMS FOR THE MILLION"

IS RESPECTFULLY DEDICATED BY THEIR HUMBLE SERVANT,

THE AUTHOR.

CONTENTS.

To my Daughter, on her fifteenth Birthday	3
"Whatever is, is right"	7
The two Sleepers	12
The chief Mourner	15
The Drunkard's Dream	19
Heaven	26
The Irish Frenchman	29
Faith	34
The Tinker's Mistake	38
To a Skull in our Sanctum	44
The Human Heart	48
Creep close to my Heart, O my Darling!	50
God bless our Home	52
A "Capital" Theme	54
The Outcast	57
Beautiful Bessie	62
Tribute to Woman	65
"I don't care!"	68
The honest working Girl	71

When Friends prove false	74
If you can't praise your Neighbor, don't name him at all	76
Perhaps so, but I doubt it	78
Should Fortune frown	81
The Cuban Volunteer's Farewell	84
Send the little Ones happy to Bed	87
A Christmas Carol	89
Kiss me good-night, Darling	91
A Word in Anger spoken	93
"I can't!" and "I'll try"	96
Lines	99
Come back to me	101
A Plea for Cuba	103
Be humble	105
A Child's Song of Praise	107
A Wanderer's Prayer	110
The Poor Man's Song	112
Plain Talk	114
Take it easy!	116
The Bouquet-Girl	118
Friendless Nelly	120
Crazy Estelle	123
Heart-Hunger	125
Twilight Musings	127
You'll weep when I am dead	130
The Bible	132

Contents.

The Power of Steam	134
The Wail of the Betrayed	137
The Difference	139
He did not read the News	142
Birds were not made in vain	148
The Kernel and the Nut	152
Have Charity	155
Starvation	157
The Hero Sailor	159
Peace, be still!	163
World-weary	165
The Beggar-Girl's Complaint	167
Elsie's Death	171
The Old Knickerbocker's Song	174
The Fireman's Death	177
Lines on the Death of a young Lady who died only four Weeks after Marriage	179
Religion	181
Rat, the Newsboy	185
What are the sad Waves saying?	191
To the Baby	194
Life and Death	196
Spoil the Rod and spare the Child	199
Be kind to your Mother	201
Why art thou cold?	204
To my Sister in California	206

Contents.

Carrier's Address	210
Alone among the Shadows	222
To Hate	224
Here's a Health to those who love us	226
He's ten Years old to-day	228
All born in October	230
Hard Luck	232
The Willow	237
Meagher's Escape	240
Shall we know those who love us?	243
The Felon's last Night	245
What is Life?	250
The Lass of Clover Lane	252
The Horse	255
Come to me, Darling	258
The Drunkard	260
A Christmas Story	263

POEMS.

TO MY DAUGHTER, ON HER FIFTEENTH BIRTHDAY.

'Tis fifteen years ago to-day
   Since Heaven sent to me
A winsome, blue-eyed baby-girl,
   As sweet as she could be.
And when I took her in my arms,
   Her cherub face to view,
I felt a strange, ecstatic joy
   That thrilled me through and through.

I watched my darling as she grew,
   So artless, pure, and mild,

To My Daughter.

And sometimes sighed to think that she
   Could not remain a child.
But now that fifteen sunny years
   Have fled since she was born,
She seems as much a babe to *me*
   As on her natal morn.

And thus I think 'twill ever be
   As on the seasons roll—
The babe will still remain a babe
   While tarries here my soul.
Yet, should she live, the time must come
   When *she* will surely see
A woman in her looking-glass,
   Whate'er *my* thoughts may be.

And when that time does come, I know
   Her mirror will reveal
The face of one whose character
   Is bright as polished steel.

To My Daughter.

She'll be as full of love and faith,
    And pure as she is now,
And virtue's self will sit enthroned
    Upon my darling's brow.

'Tis true she'll find life's pathway strewn
    With thorns as well as flowers,
And she, when sorely pierced, may sigh
    For childhood's happy hours.
But whether she be filled with joy,
    Or 'neath the chastening rod,
She'll have the same dislike for wrong,
    The same sweet trust in God.

My darling, O my darling!
    As time speeds on his way,
You'll find another love than mine,
    To comfort you some day—
A deep and thrilling sentiment
    Which you will think divine—

To My Daughter.

A love that may be more intense,
    But not more true than mine.

'Tis right that you should make new friends,
    As through the world you glide—
I can not hope to keep you, love,
    Forever at my side
'Tis right that you should form new ties—
    'Tis nature's great behest—
Nor would I clip thy wings, sweet dove,
    To keep thee in my nest.

But this I know—whate'er your lot—
    Wherever you may rove—
You'll still possess, in all its depth,
    A father's holy love.
Whether beneath the parent wing,
    Or on life's troubled sea,
God bless my bonny, blue-eyed girl,
    Wherever she may be!

"WHATEVER IS, IS RIGHT."

Disturbed in mind, and racked by pain,
   In solitude I sit,
A victim to the sombre thoughts
   That through my fancy flit;
I'm thinking of the thousand ills
   That human pleasures blight;
Yet through my musing runs this truth,
   "Whatever *is*, is right."

I see the honest toiler steeped
   In poverty and woe,
While past him struts the guilty wretch,
   Whose coffers overflow.
I see beneath religion cloaked
   Foul passions black as night;

Whatever is, is Right.

Yet in my heart I feel the truth,
   "Whatever *is*, is right."

I've seen the trembling culprit
   A justice stand before,
And heard the doom which followed
   An infringement of the law;
I knew the stern-browed magistrate
   Was vile in heaven's sight;
And yet I whispered to myself,
   "Whatever *is*, is right."

The Great, All-wise, Omnipotent,
   Who sends the gentle dew
To bless and fructify the earth,
   Sends hail and tempest too.
Behind the lowering, angry clouds
   The sun is shining bright,
And we must take them in their turn—
   "Whatever *is*, is right."

Whatever is, is Right.

I would not be misunderstood—
   I take no skeptic view,
I feel that I'm responsible
   For all which I may do.
But He who fashioned me in love,
   Will judge me not in spite,
But pity while he punishes—
   "Whatever *is*, is right."

When passions slumbering in my soul,
   By fate to flame are fanned,
He knows what my temptation is,
   How much I can withstand.
And if I fall while struggling,
   Or conquer in the fight,
He'll deal with me as I deserve—
   "Whatever *is*, is right."

The world is full of good and ill,
   And it is better so;

For if we never suffered pain,
   How could we pleasure know?
We should not prize the glorious sun
   If 'twere not for the night,
And love shows best opposed to hate—
   "Whatever *is*, is right."

And if the All-wise wills that I
   Should sorrow's chalice drain—
If he should change my hours of bliss
   To misery and pain—
Nay, should he choose to plunge my soul
   In realms of endless night,
I still should trust him, for I know
   "Whatever *is*, is right."

Then let us take the good and ill,
   Contented still to know
That greatest blessings often
   From severest trials flow.

And if we sometimes faint and fall
  Beneath temptation's might,
God's mercy still envelopes us—
  "Whatever *is*, is right."

THE TWO SLEEPERS.

An old man sat in his easy-chair,
  Where he had sat before,
Day after day, at eventide,
  For years at least a score.
The Bible open on his lap,
  A smile upon his face—
And round his brow a halo shone,
  Evolved by inward grace.

He heeded not the little one
  Who sported round his knee,
And twitched the tassel of his gown,
  And shouted out with glee,
"Come, grandpa, put your book away—
  'Tis nine o'clock you know,

And you must play awhile with me,
　　Before to bed you go.

"What! won't you play?" the child went
　　　　on
　　With disappointed air;
"You said you would at nine o'clock—
　　Grandpa, that isn't fair!
But never mind—you're tired perhaps—
　　And I'm a saucy thing—
So sit you still, and I your pipe
　　Will from the mantel bring!"

And yet the good old man stirred not,
　　Nor looked he at the child,
Who laid her head upon his book,
　　Gazed up at him and smiled:
And then she pouted pettishly,
　　And then began to weep,

And then, tired out, her eyelids closed,
  And she fell fast asleep.

And thus they slumbered tranquilly,
  The grandsire and the child;
And as they slept, it seemed as if
  They on each other smiled.
But while the red-cheeked joyous child
  The sleep of health was taking,
The old man was reposing in
  The sleep that knows no waking.

He had passed away e'en while he dwelt
  Upon the sacred story,
And left this sin-embittered life
  For one of brightest glory.
O picture rare! O lesson stern!
  For heedless man intended—
The wee child starting on the voyage
  The grandsire old had ended.

THE CHIEF MOURNER.

'Twas eve—a glorious eve!
The bright stars sparkled in the expanse above,
Like jewels in a kingly garb of blue,
And the round moon with its soft and holy light,
Looked sadly down upon this giddy world.
The zephyr, wafted from the balmy south,
Kissed the sweet flowers and whispered to the leaves,
Whose emerald faces bowed
In homage to their unseen king,
Who, gayly singing on his wanton way,
Called forth the ripples from the limpid lake
To join him in his gleeful happy song.

The whippowill, sweet minstrel of the twilight
    gray,
Poured forth her piteous, melancholy plaint,
And insect voices mingled with her note,
All joining in a vesper hymn
Which fell upon the holy hush of night
Like sweetest strains from a celestial choir.

Bathed in the moon's soft light the village
    churchyard lay,
Its marble tablets standing cold and still
Above the swelling mounds,
Fit emblems of the frigid, pulseless forms which
    lay beneath
In the calm, quiet sleep of silent death.
No more the slaves of avarice, pride, and black
    revenge—
No more the weary toilers up the hill of
    fame—
No more the zealous serfs of proud ambition,

But freed, forever freed, from all the passions
    wild
Which make this life a burden and a curse.

Beneath the drooping branches of a willow tree
There is a new-made grave.
No stone as yet uprears its marble front
To tell who sleeps below;
For but a few brief hours have passed
Since mourning friends stood round the solemn
    spot,
To see the sleeper placed within his narrow bed.
They saw him gently laid to rest, and then,
With eyelids wet, and heavy hearts, departed
To eulogize his virtues—*and forget him.*

Not all, however, will so careless prove;
For 'mid his mourners one there was
Who did not leave the spot.

Motionless he stood till the sad rites were ended,
And then, when all were gone,
He stretched himself upon the piled-up earth,
And, with one mighty sigh of grief,
Gave up the life which now he did not value.
And there he lies prone on the damp, cold clay,
True to the last—chief mourner he of all.
And yet no stone will ever mark his grave,
For he is but a dog—a huge Newfoundland dog—
Who loved the dead with so intense a love
That the barbed shaft which laid his master low
Pierced his great heart as well,
And so he fell a martyr to affection.
"All that a man hath will he give for his life."
Hero hath freely given his life for love!

THE DRUNKARD'S DREAM.

The drunkard lay on his bed of straw
   In a poverty-stricken room—
And near him his wife and children three
Sat shivering in their misery
   And weeping amid the gloom.

And as he slept, the drunkard dreamed
   Of happy days gone by,
When he wooed and won a maiden fair,
With rosy cheeks and golden hair,
   And heavenly, soft-blue eye.

Again he wandered near the spot
   Where Mary used to dwell,
And heard the warbling of the birds
   His darling loved so well,

And caught the fragrance of the flowers
　　That blossomed in the dell.

Again he at the altar stood
　　And kissed his blushing bride,
And gazing on her beauty, felt
　　His bosom swell with pride,
And thought no prince could rival him,
　　With Mary at his side.

The drunkard's wife is brooding o'er
　　The happy long ago—
In mute despair she sighs and rocks
　　Her body to and fro.
He *dreams* — she *thinks* — yet both their thoughts
　　In the same channel flow.

But now upon the drunkard's brow
　　A look of horror dwells,

And of his fearful agony,
  Each feature plainly tells—
Some hideous scene which wakes despair,
  His dream of bliss dispels.

Upon him glares a monster now
  With visage full of ire,
And yelling fiends with ribald songs
  Replace the feathered choir,
And the pure water of the spring
  Is turned to liquid fire.

And as the red flames leap and roar
  Around the brooklet's brink,
The fiends a flaming goblet raise
  And urge the wretch to drink,
While overhead the stars fade out
  And all is black as ink.

"Drink, comrade, drink!" the demons cry.
"Come to our banquet—come!
This is the fitting draught for those
    Who sell their souls for rum!"
No word the drunkard speaks, but stares
    As he were stricken dumb.

And now they point him to the brook,
    And cry, "See, drunkard! see!
Amid yon flames are struggling
    Your wife and children three,
And in their terror and despair,
    They call for help on thee!"

He rushed to aid them, but at once
    The demons blocked his way,
And then he sank upon his knees
    In agony, to pray;
But palsied was his tongue, and he
    Could no petition say.

The Drunkard's Dream.

The drunkard writhed and from his brow
   Cold perspiration broke,
As round the forms of those he loved.
   Curled up the flame and smoke,
And, shrieking in his agony,
   The wretched man awoke.

He glared around with frenzied eyes—
   His wife and children three
Sat shivering in their tattered rags
   In abject misery,
And wept outright to look upon
   His waking agony.

A pause—a sigh—and reason's light
   Again did on him beam,
And springing to his feet, he cried,
   "Thank God, 'twas but a dream,
And I, perhaps, may yet regain
   My fellow-man's esteem!"

Then reaching forth his trembling hand,
    He from the table took
A mother's gift when he was wed—
    The good God's Holy Book;
And while his loved ones knelt around,
    A solemn vow he took.

"So help me God, I ne'er again
    Will touch the poisoned bowl
Which ruins health and character,
    And steeps in guilt the soul,
And swells the fearful list of names
    Affixed to Satan's scroll!

"Help me, O Lord! to keep this oath—
    To shun each vicious den
Wherein I'd feel the tempter's power
    To make me sin again!"
And from his sobbing wife's white lips
    Arose a loud "Amen!"

The Drunkard's Dream.

And then on her wan visage beamed
    A smile of joy once more,
And, clinging to her husband's neck,
    She kissed him o'er and o'er,
And wept such happy tears as she
    Had never wept before.

*   *   *   *   *

He kept his oath, and from that time
    Their home did heaven seem;
No discord now—sweet peace was theirs,
    And love their only theme.
And daily both gave thanks to God
    Who sent the Drunkard's Dream.

HEAVEN.

The world is beautiful; but I
Can see in all beneath the sky,
Proof that the Great Divinity
   Designed that mortals,
To taste of perfect bliss, must fly
   To heaven's portals.

If not, why are our natures tried
By longings all unsatisfied?
Why do our towers, reared with pride,
   Totter and fall?
Why are the sweets on life's wayside
   Mingled with gall?

Music and discord mingle here—
The joyous laugh, the bitter tear,
The sunshine and the storm-cloud drear,
  All in an hour,
By turns will crush the heart or cheer—
  Such is earth's dower!

But there's a land beyond the sky
Where hope within us can not die,
Where there is neither tear nor sigh,
  Nor strife, nor terror;
Where all is peace and harmony,
  Unmixed with error.

There, bathed in light, we'll stand before
The One who human sorrows bore;
Who, houseless, famished, sick, and sore,
  Was yet man's friend;
And will be when this life is o'er,
  Time without end.

O glorious home! O mansion blest!
Thou recompense for life's unrest!
Close to the Saviour's bosom prest,
   How sweet to be
Loved, pitied, comforted, caressed,
   Eternally!

THE IRISH FRENCHMAN.

An English ship, by some mischance,
Once foundered on the coast of France;
But all her crew—at least a score
Of stalwart sailors—reached the shore.

At first, of course, they could but fret;
But sailors are a jolly set,
And seldom long will entertain
A grief on either land or main.

So, when they'd mourned an hour or two,
With one consent the hapless crew
Ceased murm'ring and began to think
About securing food and drink

Ere long they plenty had to eat—
A good supply of fish and meat—
But how to cook it knew they not,
Since they had neither pan nor pot.

Soon spoke the captain, with a cheer,
"See yonder smoke! A cot is near
Where we could borrow what we seek,
If we'd a man who French could speak."

"Spake Frinch!" a sailor quick replied—
An Irishman named Pat McBride—
"I learned the language years ago,
While I was shtopping at Bordeaux!"

"Have patience, byes dear, ivery one,
While I to yonder cabin run,
And in a jiffy yez'll see,
I'll bring a griddle back wid me!"

Away he bounded, like a deer,
And when he drew the cottage near,
A gray-haired Frenchman he espied,
Who stood the cabin door beside.

"Och, polly voo Fransay, monseer!"
He said, with a complaisant leer.
"Oui, monsieur!" the man replied,
As he the sailor keenly eyed.

"Well, thin, a griddle I would borrow—
I'll let yez have it back to-morrow.
Perhaps I'll fetch it back before"—
The Gaul replied, "*Je n'entends pas !*"*

"It isn't yer long tongs I wish,"
Said Pat. "I want to cook some fish.

* "I don't understand!" Pronounced "Zhar nontong par."

Me friends are yonder on the shore."
The Frenchman said, "*Je n'entends pas!*"

Pat stopped awhile and scratched his head,
And then again he loudly said,
"Och, polly voo Fransay—d'ye hear?"
The Gaul replied, "*Oui, monsieur!*"

Poor Paddy now began to rant—
"Your griddle, not your tongs, I want!
So bring it out, and hould yer jaw!"
The Gaul replied, "*Je n'entends pas!*"

"D'ye mind!" said Pat, in accents gruff,
"I've borne your nonsense long enough—
And I'll not bear it any more!"
Still cried the Gaul, "*Je n'entends pas!*"

"Take that!" cried Paddy, with a frown,
As he the hapless Gaul knocked down;

But still the astonished man did roar,
"*Je n'entends pas! Je n'entends pas!*"

Back to his comrades Paddy flew,
And soon around him flocked the crew—
"What luck! What luck, Pat?" cried they all.
"Troth," answered Pat, "no luck at all!

"Byes, dear, d'ye see, we've fallen among
    Frinchmen who can't shpake their own tongue;
Bedad, to me it seems a riddle,
They say 'long tongs' instead of griddle!"

MORAL.

My moral plainly all can see—
No one should a pretender be;
For mere pretense, when put to test,
Is worse than ignorance confessed.

FAITH.

O Thou! who holdest in thy mighty grasp
The wide-spread waters of the boundless deep,
Whose blessed smile is in the sunshine seen,
Whose awful power awakes the fearful storm,
Who scattereth o'er the mantle of the night
The glittering gems that meet our upward gaze,
Whose voice comes to us in the zephyr's breath,
And greets us in the wild tornado's roar,
Whose glorious handiwork o'er all the earth is seen
In every plant that at thy bidding grows
To please the eye or furnish needful food—
In every bird that skims the ether blue,

To charm the ravished ear with songs of praise—
In every beast that roams the forest wild,
Or with meek patience toils for thankless man—
Thou Infinite! whose presence in all space is felt,
At once mysterious, awful, grand, sublime, and beautiful,
If I, a dying, worthless clod of earth,
Might dare to lift an humble prayer to thee,
I'd ask that thou wouldst teach me what I am,
And save me from the touch of vanity and pride,
Those twin fiends who, since the first angel fell,
Have lured weak, yielding man to misery and woe.
Save me, O Father! from the skeptic tempter's power,

Who, with his specious reasoning, would sap my
    faith—
And since I can not thy dread essence analyze,
And make thee palpable to touch and sight,
Let me adore thee as a little child,
Who can not reason; but who yet can feel
Thy presence when he kneels to thee in
    prayer.
I pray for faith, O Father! Faith to feel
That thou art with me in this mortal strife—
Faith to believe that if misfortune lays
Her heavy hand on my devoted head,
'Tis done for some wise end known but to thee—
Faith to believe if earthly friends desert,
If loved and trusted ones fly from my side,
That thou wilt closer draw, and give that
    peace
Which none here can bestow nor take away—
Faith to perceive thy hand in all that may
    befall,

And to exclaim in reverence and love,
"It is the Lord, and I am still content!"
O glorious faith! O sweet and heavenly trust!
Be with me to the end, and bear my soul,
In confidence and peace, to its eternal home!

THE TINKER'S MISTAKE.

ATTENTION, friends, and I will tell
What once a luckless wight befell—
A traveling tinker, named John Drew,
Who daily tramped the country through.

A shiftless vagabond was John,
Who little recked how he got on;
Enough to eat, a bed when tired,
Was all the wealth which he desired.

And, then, to give the man his due,
He was to friendship firm and true;
His motto was, "Man is my brother,
And one good turn deserves another."

Alert he was, and wide awake;
But once he made a sad mistake,
Which bowed him down with shame and grief,
From which he vainly sought relief.

Thus runs the story: John, one day,
Had tramped a long and weary way,
When a neat road-side inn he saw,
And panting halted at the door.

"Landlord," John cried, "my worthy friend,
Any old pots or pans to mend?"
"Yes," said the host with clouded brow,
"But money's rather scarce just now."

"I want no cash," the tinker said;
"For supper, breakfast, and a bed,
I'll do the work, and think it fun."
"Done!" cried the landlord, "double done!"

The tinker labored with a will,
And backed by honesty and skill,
Ere scarce one toilsome hour had sped,
He'd finished, supped, and gone to bed.

John Drew enjoyed his night's repose,
And in the morning he arose,
And having breakfasted, he sped
Unto the worthy host, and said,

"Landlord, my warmest thanks are due
For the great kindness shown by you;
You certainly can keep an inn
As well as I can patch up tin.

"But still it does not seem to pay,
And you should find some other way
To help increase your slender store,
And keep the gaunt wolf from your door."

"The inn pays not," the landlord said,
"But then I have another trade.
I am the village glazier here,
And all *that* brings is profit clear."

"Well, good luck to you!" uttered John,
As with his budget he trudged on;
"I sha'n't forget, my generous brother,
That one good turn deserves another!"

Deep gratitude felt stout John Drew,
The feeling thrilled him through and through,
And as the village church he passed
A brilliant idea held him fast.

He paused awhile in thought profound,
Then cast a cautious glance around;
Then muttered firmly, "I will do it,
E'en though I'm caught and made to rue it!"

Then picking up a stone, John Drew
A window sent it crashing through;
And then stone after stone delivered
Till every pane of glass was shivered.

Back to the inn went John once more,
And soon the landlord stood before,
And striving hard his mirth to smother,
Cried, "One good turn deserves another!

"You gave me work my bread to earn,
And I the favor now return;
O generous host! upon my soul
No window in the church is whole.

"I've smashed each one, kind friend, and **you**
Will soon have work enough to do.
For you're a glazier, and you know
The work won't from the village go!"

The landlord glared at John amazed;
Then like one by misfortune crazed,
He caught him by the throat and swore
Such oaths as ne'er were heard before.

Wretch!" he exclaimed, "why did you so?
Your *kindness* works my overthrow!
I am the only glazier here,
But keep the church whole by the year!"

MORAL.

My moral plainly has this end:
Take no wrong means to help a friend.
For if from right's clear path you swerve,
You'll hurt the cause you fain would serve.

TO A SKULL IN OUR SANCTUM.*

THOU loathsome, grinning, hideous thing,
   So terrible to view—
Reminder of the dread, grim king!
   Is't possible that you
Once talked, and sang, and laughed with glee,
   As I do sometimes now,
With signs of pain and ecstasy
   By turns upon thy brow?

How didst thou fall? What caused thy death?
   Were thy loved kindred near

---

* This poem was published some years since under a *nom de plume.*

To a Skull in our Sanctum.

To see thee draw thy latest breath—
   Thy dying words to hear?
Or didst thou perish far from home,
   With not a fond one by,
To breathe above your lonely tomb
   A sympathetic sigh?

What were thy qualities? and what
   Thy station in this life?
Didst dwell within an humble cot,
   Far from the city's strife?
Or didst thou in the busy mart
   Day after day appear,
Striving by every wile and art
   To heap up treasure here?

Perchance thou wert a man of law,
   And practiced at the bar;
Or else, perhaps, a man of war,
   With many an ugly scar;

Or didst thou sail upon the deep
   Thy livelihood to gain?
Or didst thou some vile hell-hole keep,
   Thy base life to maintain?

Or didst thou strut thy weary hour
   Upon the mimic stage?
Or didst thou lend thy mental power
   To the historic page?
Or didst thou play a poet's part,
   And in thy language pure
Speak hope to the despairing heart,
   And comfort to the poor?

I can not tell what thou *hast* been,
   But I know what thou *art*—
A loathsome thing, whose hideous grin
   Strikes terror to the heart.

I also know that when my soul
   The better land flies to,
But a few months will onward roll
   Ere I will look like you.

THE HUMAN HEART.

Thou knowest the heart, O Father!
   And only thou canst know
Its trials and temptations—
   Its silent, secret woe.
No eye can scan its working,
   Great Spirit, save thine own!
Its innermost recesses
   Are known to thee alone!

Thou knowest the heart, O Father!
   The lines of baleful sin
Will seldom mark the human face
   E'en while it lurks within.
And there are those who walk the earth
   From all suspicion free,

Who, when thy jewels are made up,
   Will have no part in thee.

Thou knowest the heart, O Father!
   Thou all its faults can see!
And thou wilt read it truly,
   And judge it tenderly
And many a mourning sinner,
   By man despised and banned,
May, when his deeds are reconned,
   Be found at thy right hand.

Thou knowest the heart, O Father!
   Thou King all kings above!
And we may safely trust thee,
   For thou art love—*all* love!
O glorious truth! O solace!
   How vain were human bliss,
If only man could judge us,
   And there were no world but this!

CREEP CLOSE TO MY HEART, O MY DARLING.

(DESIGNED FOR MUSIC.)

Creep close to my heart, O my darling!
   And put up your lips for a kiss,
And tell me what joy in existence
   Can equal a moment like this?
I know that time flies while I clasp thee,
   But on let his chariot roll;
While near thee, he loses his power,
   Thou life-giving light of my soul!

Creep close to my heart, O my darling!
   I envy no king on his throne,
While thus in sweet rapture I hold thee,
   My dear one! my treasure! my own!

Oh! what would the world be without thee?
   Who else could my lone heart delight?
How 'twould darken my life should I lose thee,
   Thou day-star that rose on my night!

Creep close to my heart, O my darling!
   And tell me thy hopes and thy fears;
And shouldst thou feel sorrow while talking,
   I'll soon kiss away thy bright tears.
Come, tell me again that you love me,
   That nothing shall tear us apart,
While I banish thy fears with my kisses—
   Thou radiant queen of my heart!

"GOD BLESS OUR HOME!"

"God bless our home!" is my orison tender,
When the bright sun gilds the east with his splendor.
All through the darksome night while we were sleeping
Angels a watch o'er our household were keeping.

"God bless our home!" As the bright day advances
Every new blessing our calm joy enhances.
Mercy and goodness still rise up before us—
Heaven's dear angels still spread their wings o'er us.

"God bless our home!" when approaches the even,
And the bright stars gem the blue vault of heaven;
By day and by night on our heads are descending
Rich tokens of grace from a love never-ending.

"God bless our home!" O Great Spirit supernal!
Keep alive in our bosoms a passion fraternal;
Let thy love be the beacon to guard and to guide us,
And then only death can annoy or divide us.

A "CAPITAL" THEME.

The burning rays of the midday sun
   Pour down on the city's pave,
And 'neath its glare full many a one
   Is hastening to the grave.
While Mammon sits in her cool retreat,
   Far from the town's turmoil,
And cries with glee, "The dust and heat
   Were made for the sons of toil!
      Their muscle and bone
      Are mine alone—
        I use them at my will—
      And what care I
      How fast they die,
        If they my coffers fill?"

A "Capital" Theme.

A laborer from the giddy height
    Of a ladder's topmost round,
Struck by the sun-ray's scorching blight,
    Comes toppling to the ground.
And Capital takes of his wine a sup,
    While looking on with a frown,
And says, "Our tenements must go up
    If laborers do come down!"
            Their muscle and bone, etc.

A widow, wild with grief, bends o'er
    The corpse of a stalwart man,
Who but a little while before
    His earthly course had ran.
And Capital, viewing the woman's distress,
    Cries out in a tone of ire,
"Canals and railroads must progress
    If laborers do expire!"
            Their muscle and bone, etc.

Again, what dreadful sight has made
   That mother's cheek to blench?
Her son has dug with pick and spade
   A grave as well as a trench!
And Capital cries, with mirthful eyes,
   "Oh! ho! my workers brave,
Delve if you die the death, for I
   Must surely trenches have!"
         Your muscle and bone, etc.

"Ye are all the slaves of my potent will,
   As well as your babes and wives,
And I would not nourish your worth and
   skill,
   Not even to save your lives!
Ye shall fetch, and carry, and dig, and hew,
   Beneath the broiling sun,
Or ye shall starve—now which will ye do?—
   For mercy I have none!"
         Your muscle and bone, etc.

THE OUTCAST.

(AN "OW'RE TRUE TALE.")

A YOUTH sat weeping silently,
   And on his woful face,
Once innocent, might now be seen
   The shadow of disgrace.
He'd fallen from his high estate,
   And sought for peace in vain.
"My reputation's gone!" he cried,
   "I ne'er can smile again!"

But as he shed in bitterness
   The penitential tear,
His friends approached, and soothing words
   They whispered in his ear.

They bade him blot from memory's page
    The past, and keep in view
The future only, that he might
    Commence his life anew.

He did so, and a little while
    His soul was pure and free
From evil thoughts, temptation's power,
    And all unchastity.
But soon by guilty pleasure's shaft
    Again his heart was riven;
Once more he fell, but by his friends
    He was once more forgiven.

And there was one, through all his guilt,
    Forever at his side,
Who strove with more than human love
    His glaring faults to hide.

In every dark and stormy time
   A sister near him stood,
Beseeching him to shun the ill,
   And learn to choose the good.

A year rolled by, and in that time,
   Lamentable to tell,
The victim of a ruthless fiend
   That trusting sister fell.
"She loved not wisely, but too well;"
   And was her fault forgiven?
Had she a friend to counsel *her?*
   Not one, except in heaven.

The very brother that her voice
   Had pleaded most to save,
Heaped curses on her hapless head
   And wished her in the grave.
The father who had seen her grow
   In beauty 'neath his eye,

Addressed her as a loathsome wretch,
   And cast her forth to die.

Bleak was the night, and as she walked
   Along the frozen street,
The outcast trembled as she felt
   The icy, chilling sleet.
She reached a lofty edifice,
   Made the hard porch her bed—
And as she sought the sleep of death,
   "Forgive him, God," she said.

Next morning when the daylight broke,
   Her stiffened corpse was found,
And hurriedly 'twas taken up
   And put beneath the ground.
No prayer was said, no tear was shed
   When she was laid in earth,
And he who wrought her fall is thought
   A gentleman of worth.

Now, why is this? Should not the wretch
   Who tramples in the dust
A young heart's purest offering,
   Forever be accursed?
Should he not be compelled to feel
   The world's severest ban,
And meet the undisguised contempt
   Of every honest man

The wretched one who fell from grace
   In Galilee of yore,
Was told by Him who died for us
   To go and sin no more.
But now, if woman steps aside,
   Society will cry,
"Sin on—there is no hope for thee!
   Sin ever till you die!"

BEAUTIFUL BESSIE.

(DESIGNED FOR MUSIC.)

Beautiful Bessie, young, joyous, and sweet
As the flowers that bloom in her sylvan retreat,
Is weaving a coronet, fragrant and gay,
For she has been chosen as Queen of the May.
Yet she heeds not the rosy-cheeked youth who stands near
And timidly whispers his love in her ear;
A beau from the city has turned her weak head,
And she laughs at the rustic who asks her to wed.

Chorus—O wicked vanity!
    Fatal insanity!
      What will it cost?

Pride has o'erpowered her!
Sin has devoured her!
Bessie is lost!

Beautiful Bessie, once Queen of the May,
Has thrown her sweet wreath of fresh flowers away,
And changed her old home and her humble attire—
Denied her low birth and resolved to climb higher.
And now in a mansion of glitter and show
She drinks in the words of her grand city beau;
Gay is the laughter that breaks from her lips,
Bright are her eyes as the clear wine she sips.

Chorus—O wicked vanity!
Fatal insanity!
What will it cost?

> Pride has o'erpowered her!
> Sin has devoured her!
> Bessie is lost!

Beautiful Bessie is out on the street;
Cold blows the night breeze, and sharp is the sleet;
But the rude tempest brings with it no smart,
'Tis not so keen as the storm in her heart.
Brief was her gay dream, and when she awoke,
Sad was her waking—her trusting heart broke.
And ere another day glides o'er head,
Beautiful Bessie will sleep with the dead.

> *Chorus*—O wicked vanity!
> Fatal insanity!
> What has it cost?
> Pride has o'erpowered her!
> Sin has devoured her!
> Bessie is lost!

TRIBUTE TO WOMAN.

A HEALTH to the lass with the laughing blue eye,
That seems to have borrowed its hue from the sky—
Where young love is constantly feeding his flame,
And virtue sits blocking the entrance to shame.
Who weeps with the mourning and laughs with the gay,
Who can comfort old age or with infancy play,
Who quarrels with no one, but sticks to her creed—
Here's to her, for she is a woman indeed!

And here's to the girl with the lustrous black eye,
Who one moment may laugh and the next moment sigh;

Whose heart is a casket of joy and of grief,
And the first knows no limit, the last no relief.
Who deeply doth love, but as deeply can hate—
A Christian, and yet a believer in fate—
Who for pity will weep, or in anger will kill—
Here's her health—she is one of the softer sex still!

Here's to the coquette with the optic of gray,
Who will never say yes, but can hardly say nay;
Who falls dead in love with each gay beau she sees,
But can never find one for a long time to please.
Who is anxious to marry, and yet is afraid;
Who lives a young ninny, and dies an old maid;
Though blameful her follies it must be confessed,
Yet her health—she's a woman as well as the rest.

In fine, here's to woman—the large and the small,
The lean and the fleshy, the short and the tall,
The dark eye, the blue eye, the hazel and gray,
The cheerful and sullen, the grave and the gay.
I care not how faulty their natures may be—
They are women—which fact is sufficient for me;
As mother, friend, sister, maid, widow, or wife,
They are God's best gift to man, the consolers of life.

"I DON'T CARE!"

"I don't care!" How many troubles
    From these hateful words have sprung
Far too often falls the sentence
    From the lips of old and young.
How it lowers man's true standard!
    How it hurries to despair!
Spleen, and spite, and hate are nourished
    In the baleful "I don't care!"

"I don't care!" Oh! why so common
    Should this vile expression be?
Did it ever soothe a sorrow,
    Or to flight put misery?
Did it e'er dispel a shadow,
    Or bring sunshine anywhere?

Came there ever yet a blessing
  With the spiteful "I don't care"?

Pauper, in thy wretched garret,
  Did it ever bring thee gold?
Maiden, did it mend the quarrel
  Which arose when love grew cold?
Sailor on the boundless ocean,
  Would you ever danger dare
On a ship, however worthy,
  With the captain "I don't care"?

Heart-crushed pilgrim on life's highway,
  Did it ever bring thee balm?
Toiler roused by man's injustice,
  Did it e'er thy spirit calm?
Christian reaching after heaven,
  Did it ever lead to prayer?
Parent, did thy child's amendment
  Ever follow "I don't care"?

"I don't Care!"

Many a wretch in anguish groaning,
   Racked and wasted by disease;
Many a thief his crime atoning
   In his sin-bought miseries;
Many a low-browed, ruthless murd'rer
   Doomed to dangle in the air,
Owe the climax of their follies
   To the reckless "I don't care!"

"I don't care!" Oh! let the sentence
   Never pass your lips again.
It can never bring you pleasure,
   But it may engender pain.
'Mid all Satan's vile inventions,
   None more surely can ensnare
Than the worthless, good-for-nothing,
   Stupid saying, "I don't care!"

THE HONEST WORKING GIRL.

THE air is chill, the city's pave
   Is slippery and wet;
The child of wealth and luxury
   Is wrapped in slumber yet;
The sleet and snow are rushing by
   In many an angry whirl,
While hurries to her daily toil
   The honest working girl.

No word have I 'gainst gold to say,
   If it be fairly earned;
And fairly used by rich men, who
   Sweet charity have learned.
The generous merchant may with pride
   His banner broad unfurl,

But prouder is the record of
    The honest working girl.

Her clothes, though not the finest,
    Are the best that she can wear;
Her fingers boast no diamonds,
    But her face is very fair;
Her eyes are bright, and when she smiles
    She shows her teeth of pearl;
And love dwells in the bosom of
    The honest working girl.

With wages scant the ills of life
    She's fated to endure;
And yet she manages to save
    A trifle for the poor.
At any mean or sordid act,
    With scorn her lip will curl,
For noble is the nature of
    The honest working girl.

Then treat her kindly, ye proud ones,
  Who "neither toil nor spin;"
She has to struggle very hard
  Her daily bread to win.
And he—though dressed in finest cloth—
  Would be a very churl,
Who would not, if appealed to, help
  The honest working girl.

God bless the modest, gentle ones
  Who labor day by day!
And God bless those with means to spare,
  Who help them on their way!
Ye who would, in the better land,
  Possess the priceless pearl,
Treat not with scorn, nor cold contempt,
  The honest working girl.

WHEN FRIENDS PROVE FALSE.

When friends prove false and joys depart,
   And life seems drear to thee;
When grief lies heavy on thy heart,
   Then fly, love, fly to me.
Be thou my only treasured guest,
   Of all the world the dearest, best;
While pillowed on this faithful breast,
   From pain thou shalt be free.

A selfish, sordid soul may know
   The blighting touch of care,
But hearts that feel love's genial glow,
   Are proof against despair.
So, when life's storms around us rise,
   And fate her keenest arrow tries,

We'll gaze, love, in each other's eyes,
   And read our safety there.

Let courtiers fawn on royalty,
   Well pleased a look to get,
I'd rather win a smile from thee
   Than wear a coronet.
With thee life's darkest hour is bright,
Deprived of thee, life has no light;
My heart thy throne is day and night,
   My gems thine eyes of jet.

IF YOU CAN'T PRAISE YOUR NEIGHBOR, DON'T NAME HIM AT ALL.

In our judgment of others, we mortals are prone
To talk of their faults without heeding our own;
And this little rule should be treasured by all:
"If you can't praise your neighbor, don't name him at all."

Men's deeds are compounded of glory and shame,
And surely 'tis sweeter to praise than to blame;
Perfection has never been known since the fall—
"If you can't praise your neighbor, don't name him at all."

Remember, ye cynics, the mote and the beam;
Pause in your fault-finding and ponder the theme;
Who has the least charity, quickest will fall—
"If you can't praise your neighbor, don't name him at all."

If we would endeavor our own faults to mend,
We'd have all the work to which we could attend:
Then let us be open to charity's call—
"If you can't praise your neighbor, don't name him at all."

PERHAPS SO, BUT I DOUBT IT.

Old Money Grub has piles of wealth,
  Yet toils like any digger;
Greed steels his heart and saps his health,
  But larger grows the figure.
He says religion is a lie,
  And men can do without it;
Will this pay when he comes to die?
  Perhaps so, but I doubt it.

And while old Grub hoards up his gold,
  Young Grub makes haste to spend it,
Resolved to sin till he is old—
  Then change his life and mend it.
But when age bids him right the wrong,
  Do you think he'll set about it?

Will long indulgence make him strong?
   Perhaps so, but I doubt it.

And Mrs. Grub, the miser's wife,
   Who prates of Mrs. Grundy,
And leads a very worldly life
   On every day but Sunday;
Will riches her the power give
   To conquer death or flout it?
Can she, by wishing, longer live?
   Perhaps so, but I doubt it.

And young Miss Grub, so full of airs,
   And so devoid of candor,
So fond of shirking household cares,
   So very prone to slander;
Will Heaven her petition hear,
   However loud she shout it?
Will she rejoice when death draws near?
   Perhaps so, but I doubt it.

Will strife and anger lead to peace?
   Will riches bring contentment?
Will vice, by free indulgence, cease?
   Will harsh words cure resentment?
When heaven wills that we should bear
   Misfortune, can we rout it?
And is it wisdom to despair?
   Perhaps so, but I doubt it.

SHOULD FORTUNE FROWN.

Should fortune frown,
Be not cast down;
    The sailor on the ocean,
When skies grow dark,
Prepares his bark
    To meet the storm's commotion.
And so should we.
On life's rude sea,
    Be ever up and ready
To meet each storm
That comes along
    With courage firm and steady.

Strive all you can,
Work like a man
 To compass what you would do;
Then if you fail,
At fate don't rail,
 You've done all that you could do.
Hope on, hope ever—
Dejection never
 Yet won rank or station;
And toil, though vain,
At least will 'gain
 Kind friendship's approbation.

After a shower,
The bright-hued flower
 Will only look the brighter;
So should the heart
By sorrow's smart
 Be rendered purer, lighter.

No man should fear
The ills met here,
    With providence above him;
A constant mind,
A soul resigned,
    And one true heart to love him.

THE CUBAN VOLUNTEER'S FAREWELL.

Comrades, I am surely dying,
  Home again I ne'er shall see;
Would that I had died in battle,
  But it was not so to be;
Dying in this loathsome dungeon,
  But my pain will soon be o'er;
How my failing pulse would quicken,
  Could I face the foe once more!
Death I do not fear, my brothers;
  I have met him o'er and o'er.
I would die without a murmur,
  Could I face the foe once more.

When brave, struggling Cuba called me,
  I the summons did attend;

The Cuban Volunteer's Farewell.

Tell my father, if you see him,
  I was faithful to the end.
Give this Bible to my mother;
  Since our tearful last good-by,
It has been my close companion,
  And has taught me how to die.
Death I do not fear, my brothers,
  I have faced him o'er and o'er;
I would die without a murmur,
  Could I meet the foe once more.

Now the shadows gather round me,
  And my life is ebbing fast;
Bear me, comrades, to the window,
  On the sun I'd look my last.
Farewell, now, my heart-sick brothers,
  You will join me by and by;
If you perish here, remember,
  'Tis for freedom you will die.

Death I do not fear, my brothers,
   I have faced him o'er and o'er;
I would die without a murmur,
   Could I meet the foe once more.

Fiends of Spain! Incarnate devils!
   Cuba's sons shall yet be free!
All your cruelty and venom
   Can not crush out Liberty!
Still survives the holy passion
   That has carried us thus far—
Soon will beam on the horizon
   Cuba's independence star!
Death I do not fear, my brothers,
   I have faced him o'er and o'er;
I would die without a murmur,
   Could I meet the foe once more.

SEND THE LITTLE ONES HAPPY TO BED.

Send the little ones happy to bed,
    When closes the troublesome day;
Let no harsh invective be said,
    To ruffle their minds while they pray.
Sore trials and troubles full soon
    The sweet sleep of childhood will ban;
Then let them lie joyously down,
    And cherish bright dreams while they can.

Send the little ones happy to bed,
    Though they may be mischievous and wild—
Nature seldom bestows a wise head
    On a rosy-cheeked, light-hearted child.

Send the Little Ones Happy to Bed.

Then let their glad spirits have play,
   And brighter and stronger they'll grow,
Like a stream that runs free on its way,
   And suffers no check in its flow.

Send the little ones happy to bed,
   You know not what ill may be near;
Ere the morning your pets may be dead,
   Then vain the regret or the tear.
So let them lie down with delight,
   And fail not to give and to take
A kiss when they prattle "Good night!"
   And a kiss in the morn when they wake

A CHRISTMAS CAROL.

Away with care and melancholy!
   'Tis the merry Christmas time;
'Neath the mistletoe and holly,
   We'll dance to the Christmas chime.

This is the day that Christ was born,
   And we should joyful be,
For the Saviour's natal star
Shed its blessèd beams afar
   Over lost humanity.

Praise the Saviour high in glory!
   Loudly let your anthems ring!
Oh! how wonderful the story—
   The babe is now our king!

"Good-will to men and peace on earth!"
  Our heartfelt chorus be,
Till we gain the happy shore,
Where we'll praise him evermore,
  Throughout eternity.

KISS ME GOOD NIGHT, DARLING.

THE clock has struck ten, Willie, dear, and you know
Papa has declared that at ten you must go.
Old folks are so queer! But perhaps *he* is right.
So kiss me good night, darling! Kiss me good night!

I declare 'tis eleven, and you are here still!
You know well enough *I'm* not keeping you, Will!
If you don't go at once, I must put out the light.
So kiss me good night, darling! Kiss me good night!

Kiss Me Good-Night, Darling.

'Tis twelve o'clock, now, and papa's out of bed!
Don't you hear his gruff voice and quick step overhead!
Here's your hat! Go at once! Oh! I'm in such affright!
Quick! Kiss me good night, darling! Kiss me good night!

A WORD IN ANGER SPOKEN.

A word in anger spoken—
　How often does it prove
The cause of cold indifference
　In hearts whose rule is love!
How oft the sweetest pleasures
　Humanity can know
Are by a harsh expression
　Turned into bitter woe!

A word in anger spoken—
　How many sighs, and tears,
And sleepless nights, and cheerless days,
　And weary, weary years,
Have been its mournful product,
　Though charity essayed
To heal the deadly, festering wound
　Which thoughtless anger made!

A Word in Anger Spoken.

A word in anger spoken—
    A blot upon life's page
Which oft will leave its impress
    From youth to latest age.
Man may forgive an insult;
    But still it bears its fruit,
For memory is a tyrant
    Whose rule is absolute.

A word in anger spoken
    Has oft engendered strife
Between the loving husband
    And the doting, trusting wife;
Has caused a barrier to rise
    Between the child and mother,
And led foul enmity to part
    The sister and the brother.

A word in anger spoken—
    If you have felt its blight,

Resolve henceforth to " know thyself,"
   And train thy spirit right.
Keep watch upon thy every thought,
   Thy every look and word,
And thou shalt live from sorrow free,
   As joyous as a bird.

A word in anger spoken—
   Oh! weigh the sentence well;
For it contains a lesson
   That words are vain to tell.
The human heart is faulty,
   And the wisest of us all
May drop a careless word in wrath,
   That we would fain recall.

"I CAN'T!" AND "I'LL TRY."

"I CAN'T!" exclaims the truant boy,
    While loitering on the way;
"I can't!" repeats the imbecile,
    Whose locks are streaked with gray;
"I can't!" It is the common phrase
    Of all inclined to fly
When dangers menace; but the brave
    Would rather say, "I'll try!"

"I can't!" It stultifies the soul
    And palsies all within;
'Tis made the flimsy, weak excuse
    For each besetting sin.
And many an ill that stays by us
    Away would quickly fly,

"I Can't!" and "I'll Try."

If we would hold our heads erect
  And firmly say, "I'll try!"

The drunkard says, "I can't!" when he
  Is counseled to abstain;
The sluggard drawls, "I can't!" when told
  By work his bread to gain.
The hardened thief exclaims, "I can't
  Temptation's door go by!"
But each his fault could master
  If he'd stoutly say, "I'll try!"

"I can't!" Had Fulton thus exclaimed
  When jeered at as insane;
Or bold Columbus when his crew
  Revolted on the main;
Or brave Galileo, when forced
  His theory to disown;
Or Morse, when pinched by poverty
  And struggling on alone—

Had these brave souls, and many more
   Who won the wreath of fame,
Sat down to murmur and lament
   When difficulties came,
How many blessings we should miss
   Which make us glad to-day,
And what a sombre cloud would on
   The hill of science lay.

"I can't!" Oh! drop the hateful phrase,
   Ye toilers everywhere;
Be earnest on life's battle-field,
   Fail not to do and dare!
Faint not, if stern reverses come,
   But fix your faith on high,
And let your noble motto be,
   "With God's good help, I'll try!"

LINES.

(WRITTEN IN "OUR CARRIE'S" ALBUM.)

Lustrous eyes revealing
  Young Love peeping through,
Heart of warmest feeling,
  Nature kind and true;
Lineaments which tell us
  Thou wert born to bless,
Friendship's counsel zealous,
  Gentle Carrie S.

Full of toil and sorrow
  Is this weary life,
Each succeeding morrow
  Brings its care and strife;

But may heavenly power
    Shield *thee* from distress,
Guard thee every hour,
    Trusting Carrie S.

Time may overcome thee,
    Touch thy hair with gray,
Steal thy beauty from thee,
    Take thy strength away;
But thy *soul* will never
    Lose its loveliness;
That will bloom forever,
    Truthful Carrie S.

COME BACK TO ME.

(DESIGNED FOR MUSIC.)

Too long have we been parted—
    Come back to me!
I'm lonely, broken-hearted—
    Come back to me!
I tread familiar bowers,
But scentless are the flowers,
And weary are the hours—
    Come back to me!

Think of your promise broken—
    Come back to me!
Your words of love once spoken—
    Come back to me!

Hearts truly pledged forever
No thoughtless word should sever,
The past we'll think of never—
            Come back to me!

I've loved since first I met thee—
            Come back to me!
I never can forget thee—
            Come back to me!
With looks of love I'll meet thee,
With words of love I'll greet thee;
Relent, then, I entreat thee—
            Come back to me!

A PLEA FOR CUBA.

Freemen of our great republic,
  Bend to heaven the knee—
Raise your hands and shout the chorus,
  Cuba shall be free!
Spain, vile Spain, with steel and halter,
Hovers over freedom's altar,
Cowards are we if we falter—
  Strike for liberty!

By the graves of our brave sires,
  By their great deeds done,
By sweet freedom's sacred fires
  Lit at Lexington;
By our blood-cemented nation,
By each bondman's aspiration,
By our hopes of dear salvation,
  Do not Cuba shun!

Hark! across the stormy waters
   Comes a piteous cry;
'Tis from Cuba's sons and daughters,
   "Will ye let us die?"
Freemen, up! No longer dally!
Round fair Cuba's standard rally,
From the mountain and the valley—
   Cause her foes to fly!

Shall Spain's stabbers wield the sabre,
   Flushed with victory?
God forbid! Let's pray and labor!
   Cuba *must* be free!
Clamor for her recognition,
Hurl her tyrants to perdition,
Thus may we fulfill our mission,
   Death to slavery!

BE HUMBLE.

Who glories in power? Who boasts of his might?
Who worships his gold-heaps by day and by night?
Who makes only vice-gilded pleasure his aim?
Who strives only after the chaplet of fame?

Vain mortal! Thy power and might must decay,
Thy riches take wing and fly swiftly away!
Thy dearly-bought pleasure be followed by pain,
Thy wreath of renown prove unstable and vain!

What is this existence to which we all cling?
It passes away like a bird on the wing.

'Tis a breath, 'tis a vapor, 'tis a song, 'tis a sigh,
We weep, we rejoice, we grow weary, we die!

And this ends the story—the babe of to-day
Crowds out the grandsire who passes away;
And the babe in its turn hurries on to the goal,
Where death stands awaiting the flight of the soul.

Be humble, then, mortal, thou worm of the sod,
And bend thy proud knee in contrition to God,
Who only is mighty, who only can save,
And whose smile can light up e'en the gloom of the grave.

Be humble, and patient, and ready to go
Whenever thy mission is finished below;
Then rest thee contented, no terror can come
When God in his wisdom shall summon thee home.

A CHILD'S SONG OF PRAISE.

"BLESS the Lord, O my soul! and forget not all his benefits."

At morning and at eventide,
   Father above, I call on thee
To make me pure, to check my pride,
   And teach me sweet humility.
This is my duty, but I know
   It is not all my tongue should say;
From thee all earthly blessings flow,
   And I should praise as well as pray.

Who shields me from the howling storm?
   Who watches me in slumber sweet?
Who gives me clothes to keep me warm?
   Who furnishes me with food to eat?

A Child's Song of Praise.

Who makes my limbs so lithe and free
   When with my little mates I play?
'Tis thee, O gracious God! 'tis thee.
   And I must praise as well as pray.

For father kind and mother dear,
   And friends who are so true to me,
For all the good I see and hear,
   I am indebted, Lord, to thee.
For brain to learn, and books to read,
   And grace to keep bad thoughts away;
For these, O Lord! I feel, indeed,
   That I should praise as well as pray.

And, gift all others prized above,
   Thy precious word, my hope and light,
Which fills my heart with sacred love,
   And keeps me in the path of right;
Which tells me of a Saviour dear
   Who watches o'er me night and day;

Oh! is it not, then, very clear
   That I should praise as well as pray?

Yes, while I live I'll praise the Lord,
   And daily strive in grace to grow;
Directed by his precious word,
   I'll walk where living waters flow.
Oh! praise the Lord, my soul, and raise
   And keep alive the sacred flame,
And all that is within me praise
   My gracious Maker's holy name.

A WANDERER'S PRAYER.

FATHER in heaven, when my soul
   Shall take its flight from earth,
Grant that my frame may perish on
   The soil that gave it birth;
Grant that the friends who cherished me
   In sunshine and in gloom,
Who sorrowed and rejoiced with me,
   May lay me in the tomb.

I know that when the spirit flies
   Its prison-house of clay,
The wondrous structure, cold and dead,
   Soon hastens to decay;
But though the pulseless, mouldering clod
   No sense of joy may have,

My spirit will rejoice when friends
   Assemble r'ound my grave.

I wish no monumental pile
   To mark the solemn spot,
No epitaph in fulsome style
   To tell what I was not;
But I'd have those who knew me here,
   As o'er my tomb they bend,
Say, with a feeling all sincere,
   "He was a faithful friend!"

THE POOR MAN'S SONG.

I LIVE in a garret, but what do I care?
I'm safer than some of my great neighbors are;
The loss of my wealth I'm not troubled about,
And my diet will certainly keep off the gout.
Then a truce to all grumbling, for happen what may,
While I've health, I'll be happy by night and by day.

There's old Mr. Graball, whose dwelling's hard by,
At the loss of a dollar is ready to cry;
And yet I'll be bound that the old fellow's dimes
Outnumber, by far, his quintillion of crimes.

Then a truce to all grumbling, the morsel I eat
Is honestly gotten, and wholesome, and sweet.

Then there's Mr. Freeliver, over the way,
Who groans with dyspepsia, day after day;
If Nature permitted, how quickly would he
Be willing to barter conditions with me?
Then a truce to all grumbling, for champagne, 'tis clear,
Is not so conducive to health as small-beer.

Give me but the power to labor, and then
As happy I'll be as the richest of men;
And the evils committed in grasping for gold
Can't trouble my conscience when I have grown old.
Then a truce to all grumbling, for happen what may,
While I've health, I'll be happy by night and by day.

PLAIN TALK.

O Lizzie, dear! incline your ear
   To Bob, your faithful lover,
Whose talk is plain, and who in vain
   Endeavors to discover
Your diamond eye, your spicy sigh,
   Your neck of alabaster,
And who would deem a golden curl
   A terrible disaster.

The man with cash and black mustache,
   From college, full of learning,
With body laced, by fashion graced,
   Has powerful discerning;
He sees the diamond, pearl, and gold,
   A sprite his heart is breaking,

While I see but a charming girl
   Of old Dame Nature's making.

I love thee, Lizzie, dear as life,
   But would not, were I able,
Have thee made half a mineral
   And half a vegetable.
Nor would I have thee pale and sad,
   Thy mirthfulness concealing,
But red-cheeked, lively, gay, and glad,
   A young heart's honest feeling.

Then, Lizzie, if you'll be my wife,
   Believe me, I'll endeavor
To make thee happy all my life,
   And leave thee, darling, never.
I may not be forever glad,
   But I a smile can borrow
Of thee whenever I am sad,
   And pay it on the morrow.

TAKE IT EASY!

TAKE it easy, men of muscle!
   Take it easy, men of brain!
You may stumble if you hurry,
   And you nothing then will gain.
Any work that's worth the doing
   Surely is worth doing well;
Rather than by haste destroy it,
   Better stop and breathe a spell.

Take it easy, mirthful maidens!
   Take it easy, girls and boys!
Every pleasure rashly followed,
   In the end too surely cloys.
Never haste to grasp the shadow
   When the substance is secure!

Trust me, there is health and safety
  In the motto, "Slow and sure."

Take it easy, slave of passion!
  Hasty words will nothing gain;
While your breast is filled with anger,
  All your work will be in vain.
Curb your temper till cool reason
  Has a chance to play its part,
And your task will be the easier,
  And the purer be your heart.

Take it easy, mourning pilgrim!
  Sad at heart and sick at soul,
Why shouldst thou, when heaven is certain,
  Be so swift to reach the goal?
Wait God's time, and thy probation
  On the earth will soon be o'er,
And thou'lt wrestle with temptation
  And heart-sorrow nevermore.

THE BOUQUET-GIRL.

"Bouquets!" like a mourning spirit's wail
    Arose on the midnight air,
From the lips of a girl whose features pale
    Were marked by grief and care.
Her azure eyes were dim with tears,
    No purchaser she found;
And oh! it seemed the woe of years
    Was in that plaintive sound.
Bouquets! bouquets! oh! pray do buy,
    At home there is no bread;
I hear my little brother's cry,
    And darling mother's dead!

"Bouquets!" and the poor child's tired feet
    Touched wearily the ground,

While the night wind through the lonely street
    Rushed by with a moaning sound.
"Bouquets!" in a low, despairing tone,
    While onward still she crept,
And then between a sigh and moan
    She sought a seat and slept.
Bouquets! bouquets! oh! pray do buy,
    At home there is no bread;
I hear my little brother's cry,
    And darling mother's dead.

FRIENDLESS NELLY.

(DESIGNED FOR MUSIC.)

LITTLE Nelly, pale with hunger,
   Wanders through the street,
Heavy is her heart with sorrow,
   Weary are her feet.
Penniless she journeys homeward,
   Shivering with dread,
For her father is a drunkard,
   And her mother's dead.
What a sad, sad lot for Nelly,
   Nelly meek and mild!
Heavenly Father, oh! in pity
   Shield the drunkard's child.

Nelly's eyes are large and lustrous,
　　Golden is her hair,
And she has a sweet expression,
　　Nelly's very fair.
But the child's unearthly beauty,
　　That should be her crown,
All too soon may prove the burden
　　That will drag her down.
What a sad, sad lot for Nelly,
　　Nelly meek and mild!
Heavenly Father, oh! in pity
　　Shield the drunkard's child.

Nelly's character is spotless,
　　She is pure as snow;
Can she, in the wicked city,
　　Keep forever so?
Sin, and sorrow, and temptation,
　　Still her steps pursue;

Motherless, with no adviser,
  What will Nelly do?
What a sad, sad lot for Nelly,
  Nelly meek and mild!
Heavenly Father, oh! in pity
  Shield the drunkard's child.

CRAZY ESTELLE.

(DESIGNED FOR MUSIC.)

In the great city she wanders alone;
None to befriend her—uncared for, unknown—
Muttering ever of joys that have fled,
Calling on some one who sleeps with the dead.
What her life's story is no one can tell—
She is known only as Crazy Estelle.
No one to pity her, none to caress—
God help the wanderer in her distress.

CHORUS.

No one to pity her, none to caress—
God help the wanderer in her distress!

Hopelessly lost in the city's vast throng,
Sadly she warbles a plaintive love-song;
Looking around her, but looking in vain,
For a loved face she will ne'er see again.

Wild is her dark eye and frenzied her air,
And her white brow is convulsed by despair;
But not a wicked thought enters her head,
She only seeks for a lover that's dead.

CHORUS.

No one to pity her, none to caress—
God help the wanderer in her distress!

What will become of her out in the street?
Heart-sick and foot-sore, no happy retreat;
Who will take care of her? Where can she go?
Wretched, forlorn, and o'erburdened with woe.
No one on earth can the wanderer save,
And she will only find rest in the grave.
Guard her, bright angels, where'er she may tread,
Seeking in vain for her lover that's dead.

CHORUS.

No one to pity her, none to caress—
God help the wanderer in her distress!

HEART-HUNGER.

'Tis sweet to feel in this sad world of change,
   Where selfishness and pride so much abound,
That there is one, however wide we range,
   To greet us lovingly when home is found.
One whom we know will faithful be till death,
   Whose heart-throbs play in concert with our own,
Whose love will bless us till our latest breath,
   To whose pure bosom falsehood is unknown.

The famished wretch who droops his head with shame
   May be relieved by any passer-by;
The ardent youth who hungers after fame
   Has always hope of feasting presently.

But, oh! to feel that we are all alone,
    That love's sweet cup has vapored to the lees,
That there is no heart we can call our own—
    This is a hunger nothing can appease.

To wander on without a ray of hope,
    To find no respite even in our sleep,
Life's sun extinguished, in the dark to grope,
    And hopeless through this weary world to creep;
No balm for us, no medicine can cure—
    The ailing is beyond the reach of art—
All other hunger strong men may endure,
    Except the weary, dreary hunger of the heart.

TWILIGHT MUSINGS.

'Twas twilight—the bright-plumaged birds were at rest,
And the sun in his glory had sunk in the west,
All labor had ceased, and the whippowil's song
Like a dirge from the forest came wailing along.

A maiden sat watching with wondering eye
The many-hued cloudlets that skirted the sky,
Which seemed, as they varied their colors, designed
To furnish a type of the changeable mind.

As she gazed, twilight called forth the fair stars of even,
To light with their lustre the blue vault of heaven.

And soon like a host in their silvery sheen,
The pure lamps in ether were twinkling seen.

They spangled the heavens in dazzling array,
And night drove the sober-browed twilight away;
But still the young maiden in rapture gazed there,
"O night!" she exclaimed, "thou art wondrously fair."

But e'en as she spoke, a low, murmuring plaint
Came, mildly at first, as the sigh of a saint;
Then swiftly the storm-king arose on the air,
And left but one bright star to radiate there.

"Alas!" cried the maid, "'tis a picture of life!
How often is happiness turned into strife!
Bright prospects may light us awhile, but how soon
May frowning misfortune make night of our noon!

"Yet, though grief wring the bosom and tears
    dim the eye,
One bright star at least shall illumine life's sky;
For wretched indeed must that pilgrim be
Who can 'not one pure ray of blessed hope see!"

YOU'LL WEEP WHEN I AM DEAD.

(DESIGNED FOR MUSIC.)

Smile while thou canst, be gay and unheeding,
   Riches and splendor at last are thine own;
Strive to forget that a true heart is bleeding,
   Proud in its anguish, but wretched and lone.
And when the clouds of despair hover o'er thee,
   When the false friends of thy summer have fled,
Then will my sorrowing shade flit before thee;
   False to me living, you'll weep when I'm dead

Blithesome and free in life's morning you found me,
   Sorrow had never o'ershadowed my brow;

Bright fell the sunlight of sweet peace around
    me—
Where, O thou fickle one! where is it now?
Gone! like the light on the verge of the ocean,
    Raised by false hands to allure the doomed
    bark—
Suddenly quenched 'mid the wild storm's commotion,
    Leaving the wrecked ones to grope in the dark.

Gay is thy dream, but soon comes the dawning,
    When thou'lt awaken to sorrow and shame;
Wealth fleeth like the light mists of the morning,
    And there's no bubble more empty than fame.
Ah! then, when clouds of despair hover o'er thee,
    When the false friends of thy summer have
    fled,
My mournful shade will, I know, flit before thee—
    False to me living, you'll weep when I'm dead.

THE BIBLE.

Book all other books excelling,
   Man's best earthly friend and guide,
Spring from whose pure source is welling
   Mercy in a crystal tide!
Heaven's sweet light shines all about thee,
   Making plain the way to go;
What were this sad world without thee
   But a vale of sin and woe?

God's own word! Life-giving treasure!
   Solace when all others fly!
Who thy wond'rous wealth can measure?
   Who can set thy price too high?
Grief-dispeller—heart-consoler—
   Faith-sustainer—sorrow's bane—

The Bible.

Death-destroyer—sin-controller—
   Soul-enlivener—foe to pain!

Spirit-stirrer—vision-brightener—
   Sin-expeller—sick soul's cure—
Strife-allayer—burden-lightener—
   All-wise teacher—refuge sure!
Heavenly mentor—soul-wealth bringer—
   Sinner's heart's ease—heaven's chart—
All in all—salvation-singer—
   Balm to every broken heart!

Holy Book! How all should love it!
   How its words refresh the soul!
Nothing earthly is above it—
   'Tis God's light from pole to pole.
Beauties ever new discerning
   As I con its pages o'er,
Let my soul have but one yearning—
   How to prize and love it more!

THE POWER OF STEAM.

Oh! be my theme the power of steam—
  'Tis greater than sword or pen;
For it furnishes bread, and raiment and bed,
  For millions of toiling men.
Day after day it puffs away,
  Alike in calm or storm,
And mortals gaze in mute amaze
  At what it can perform.

It winnows, it plows, it heads, it blows,
  It cuts, it slits, it dresses,
It stamps, it planes, it digs, it drains,
  It condenses, collects, and presses.
It forges, it rolls, it melts, it moulds,
  It files, it hammers, it rasps,

It punches, it beats, it cooks, it heats,
   Releases and tightly grasps.

It propels, it rows, it warps, it tows,
   It pulls, it carries, it scatters,
It pushes, it draws, it gouges, it bores,
   It polishes, breaks, and batters.
It lowers, it lifts, it grinds, it sifts,
   It washes, it smooths, it crushes,
It picks, it hews, it prints the news,
   It rivets, it sweeps, it brushes.

It sculls, it screws, it mends, it glues,
   It pumps, it irrigates,
It sews, it drills, it levels hills,
   Shuts, opens, and elevates.
It extracts, confines, it marks out lines,
   It thrashes, it separates,
It mixes, it kneads, it drives, it leads,
   It chisels, it excavates.

The Power of Steam.

It stamps, it turns, it hatches, it churns,
   It mortises, saws, and shaves,
It bolts, it brings, it lends us wings,
   It fights the winds and waves.
It scutches, it cards, advances, retards,
   It spins, it twists, it weaves,
It coins, it shears, tears down, uprears,
   Discharges and receives.

Then be my theme the power of steam—
   'Tis greater than sword or pen;
For it furnishes bread, and raiment and bed,
   For millions of toiling men.
Day after day it puffs away,
   Alike in calm or storm,
And mortals gaze in mute amaze,
   At what it can perform.

THE WAIL OF THE BETRAYED.

Come, night, sad night, and let me hide
   My wretchedness in thee!
Nurse in thy gloom my woman's pride,
   My heart's deep agony!
Thy sombre shadows suit me well,
   My trouble and unrest
Are suited to thy darksome spell—
   'Tis night within my breast.

The flowers that bloom at early morn
   To some may beauteous be,
But those that ope at night's approach
   Are dearer far to me.
The first like sunshine friends may smile
   In fortune's happy light,

The latter will our griefs beguile
    In sorrow's gloomy night.

Though bright the glorious orb of day,
    It has no charm for me;
I would not have a single ray
    Shine on my misery.
Like the crushed flower upon the plain,
    Dust-covered from the sight,
So would I hide my loathsome stain
    In everlasting night.

I love the dark-robed night, for she
    Shares all my bitter grief;
She has a sigh in every breeze,
    A tear on every leaf;
And while the moon looks sadly down,
    The stars shed, as they glow,
A ray of sorrowing light that seems
    Like sympathetic woe.

THE DIFFERENCE.

A MAIDEN who spent the weary hours
In going from house to house with flowers,
Stopped at a gorgeous mansion, where
She spread to view her bouquets rare.
Wan was her look and dim her eye,
And as she marked the passers-by,
Her youthful bosom seemed to be
The dwelling-place of misery.

A lady from out the mansion came,
A richly-costumed, pompous dame,
Whose look of vain and haughty pride
The flower-vender terrified.
She viewed the poor girl's bright-hued store,
And turned the bouquets o'er and o'er,

Then asked the price, demurred, and then
In the rich mansion went again.

The maiden, footsore, sad, and weak,
Wiped off the tear that gemmed her cheek,
And then again she passed along
Amid the city's giddy throng.
At length a bright-eyed working girl,
With ringing laugh and sunny curl,
Approached her, and in merry sport
A bunch of her sweet flowers bought.

But as the girl the money took,
The buyer marked her wretched look,
And kindly sought the cause to know
Why her young heart was touched with woe.
The girl replied, with tearful eyes,
"At home my aged mother lies;
She's ill, alone, and should be nursed,
But I must sell my flowers first."

The Difference.

The shop-girl paused and heaved a sigh,
A tear was in her clear blue eye;
She'd saved a sum to buy a shawl;
But "Here!" she cried, "I'll take them all!
My mother's dead, and doubtless she
Is looking now from heaven at me,
And she will smile—I know she will—
To see me hug her precepts still."

HE DID NOT READ THE NEWS.

One summer's morn to Gotham came
A weary wight, John Smith by name,
Who traveled hither from the West
The profit of fair trade to test.
His form was bony, lank, and tall,
His clothes were poor, his means were small.
A man he was of narrow views
Who did not care to read the news.

John entertained, 'twixt you and me,
Queer notions of economy.
At home he drank, and chewed—would go
To see the traveling circus show—
Would puff his cash away in vapor,
But couldn't afford to take a paper.

Of fresh events he held no views,
Because he didn't read the news.

Scarce had he got the city in,
Ere his misfortunes did begin;
He sold his cattle, got the cash,
And then resolved to cut a dash.
He started off without delay,
And, whistling, sauntered down Broadway,
To take an independent cruise,
He didn't care to read the news.

"Say, Johnny!" cried a voice, "look here!"
John turned and saw a stranger near.
"Why, don't you know me, Cousin John?"
The man—a well-dressed youth—went on.
"Why, I knew you at once, right well!
Come, go with me to my hotel!"
John went—he couldn't see the *ruse*—
Oh! if he had but read the news!

He did not Read the News.

No one will doubt us when we say
John's *cousin* was enriched that day,
While hapless John, of sense bereft,
Had only half his money left.
"Gosh!" cried the dupe, with rage and grief,
"A fellow dressed like that, a thief!
I swan! 'twould give a saint the blues!
Oh! don't I wish I'd read the news!"

Deploring his unhappy fate,
He to a drinking shop went straight
His sorrows in a glass to drown;
And when he'd gulped the liquor down,
At once his brain began to spin,
For what he swallowed drugged had been,
And soon his senses John did lose.
Poor dupe! He hadn't read the news.

Then many a low-browed villain came,
Considering John Smith fair game.

They plucked him bare, and not a cent
  Had he when to the Tombs he went.
"Judge!" cried the victim, "Judge! look here!
  I've lost five hundred dollars clear!
  I hope your aid you won't refuse."
"John," said the justice, "read the news!"

A sharp-eyed newsboy standing near
  Cried, "Johnny, walk off on your ear!
  Don't grumble 'cause you've lost your pelf,
  For now you know how 'tis yourself!
  You're fortunate, my old galoot,
  That some one didn't bust your snoot!
  I guess you're one o' them foo-foos
  Who never want to read the news!

"If these cops wasn't standin' by,
  I'd go to work and break your eye!
  I'd like to paste yer in the ear!
  I'd like to poultice yer! D'yer hear?

I'd like to take and warm yer jaw,
I would, if 'twasn't for the law!
I'm down on these 'ere country Jews,
Too mean to spend a cent for news!"

With heavy heart John left the court,
And quickly he his village sought,
Where safe at last, his friends flocked round,
To learn what fortune he had found.
John eyed them o'er and o'er again,
Then, with a visage full of pain,
He said, "Friends, if there's one here who's
A goin' to travel, *read the news!*

"I never have myself, but now
I'll make a solemn, earnest vow
To go, ere speeds another day,
And a full year's subscription pay.

I'll read the paper, every line,
If it takes from six o'clock till nine;
For b'lieve me, friends, a mere recluse
Is he who never reads the news."

BIRDS WERE NOT MADE IN VAIN.

A FARMER once,
A youthful dunce,
Stood gazing o'er a field
Of springing corn,
By blackbirds shorn
Of half that it should yield.
Said he, "Bright birds,
Mark ye my words,
Your doom is surely sealed.

"Ye have had your share,
Of my produce rare;
Ye have ranged my broad fields o'er,

And picked and ate
At such a rate
That half my crop or more
Has felt the blight,
Of your greedy bite,
But now your reign is o'er!"

He kept his word;
Each joyous bird
That on the morrow trilled
His joyous song
The meads along
Was mercilessly killed.
"Now," cried the lad,
With visage glad,
"My barn will sure be filled!"

Time sped along,
The blackbird's song
No more was heard in air;

The farmer stood
In solemn mood,
And features full of care.
His eye roamed o'er
The fields, but saw
No vegetation there.

On each green leaf
A reptile thief,
Erst the blithe blackbird's prey,
A full meal had·
The farmer lad
Had sent their scourge away,
And the poor wight,
Possessed not quite
The blackbird's power to slay.

He viewed the scene
With thoughtful mien,

His heart was touched with pain.
"O bright-winged birds!"
He cried, "that words
Would bring ye back again!
For now, in sooth,
I feel the truth,
Birds were not made in vain!"

THE KERNEL AND THE NUT.

"He who would eat the kernel must not complain because obliged to crack the nut."—*Old Saying.*

Ye who in this changeful life
  Not a ray of joy can see,
Ye who foster care and strife,
  Never from excitement free;
Ye who never seek for peace,
  Hoping it will seek for you,
Daily will your woes increase,
  And you'll find this maxim true:
Earthly joys and joys supernal
  From the sluggard mind are shut;
If you wish to taste the kernel,
  First you'll have to crack the nut.

Life's stream seldom smoothly flows,
    And at times we're forced to mourn;
But who would reject the rose
    Even though it has its thorn?
By hard labor we may seize
    Pleasure from the lap of pain,
If we idly take our ease,
    We shall look for joy in vain.
Earthly joys and joys supernal
    From the sluggard mind are shut;
If you wish to taste the kernel,
    First you'll have to crack the nut.

Should misfortune weigh you down,
    Never yield to dark despair;
Take the cross and win the crown,
    Toil for good and laugh at care.
Resolutely strive and plan,
    Inactivity is vain,

The Kernel and the Nut.

What would pleasure be to man
 If he never tasted pain?
Earthly joys and joys supernal
 From the sluggard mind are shut;
If you wish to taste the kernel,
 First you'll have to crack the nut.

HAVE CHARITY.

Through the great sin-blasted city
  Toils a homeless little one,
Not a friend to soothe or pity,
  Not a bed to lie upon;
Ragged, dirty, bruised, and bleeding,
  Subject still to kick and curse,
Schooled in sin and sadly needing
  Aid from Christian tongue and purse.

But the rich and gay pass by her,
  Full of vanity and pride,
And a pittance they deny her,
  As they pull their skirts aside.
Then a sullen mood comes o'er her,
  Reckless she of woe or weal,

Death from hunger is before her—
   She must either starve or steal.

She *does* steal; and who can blame her?
   Hunger-pangs her vitals gnaw,
None endeavors to reclaim her,
   And she violates the law.
Then the pampered child of fashion,
   Who refused to give relief,
Cries, with well-affected passion,
   "Out upon the little thief!"

Censors full of world-wise schooling,
   Cease to censure and deplore;
When the girl transgressed man's ruling,
   She obeyed a higher law.
Take her place, feel her temptation—
   Starved, unhoused, no succor nigh—
And, though sure of reprobation,
   Ye would steal ere ye would die!

STARVATION.

At the close of a bitter cold day,
When the snow on the frozen ground lay,
  A poor woman's child,
  With a face wan and mild,
In a garret was passing away.
    Gaunt hunger,
    Dread hunger,
Had stolen the bloom from his cheek,
  And his mother sat there,
  With a look of despair,
To catch what her darling might speak.

"Come closer, dear mother," he said,
"And lay your soft hand on my head,
  And tell me once more
  Of that other bright shore
Where we never shall hunger for bread."

"Hush, darling!
　　Peace, darling!"
She raised him to lull him to rest,
　And she brushed the soft hair
　From his forehead so fair,
But he died as he lay on her breast.

The morning broke joyous and clear,
'Twas the first of the opening year;
　But the shouts of gay boys,
　And the cannon's rude noise,
Fell unheard on that poor mother's ear.
　　Oh! hear it!
　　Oh! heed it!
Ye wealthy, well clothed, and well fed,
　In that season of joy
　A mother and her boy
Had perished for the want of bread.

THE HERO SAILOR.

Lieutenant W. Lewis Herndon, U. S. N., late commander of the U. S. Mail Steamship Central America, was lost at sea September 12th, 1857, by which disaster 326 souls perished, including Captain Herndon, and over $2,000,000 of treasure was lost.

Look at his features, ye who read
  Man's nature in his face,
And tell me if a single line
  Ignoble ye can trace.
Peruse the well-marked lineaments
  As closely as you can,
And say do they not "give the world
  Assurance of a man"?

No giant strength did he possess,
  No stalwart, towering form,

Yet with the strength of Hercules
    He wrestled with the storm;
'Twas honor nerved the hero's arm
    And stirred his lion heart,
And taught him how, at duty's call,
    With life itself to part.

"There is no hope! It can not be
    That he escaped the wreck!
For he would be the last to leave
    The fated vessel's deck!"
Thus spoke, and truly spoke,
    The gallant sailor's noble wife;
She knew to keep his honor whole
    He'd sacrifice his life.

Weep for his fate, ye maidens,
    Wives, and mothers of the land!
On history's page eternally
    The glorious truth shall stand,

That in that fearful hour of death
   Upon the ocean wild,
Of all on board there was not lost
   A woman or a child.

'Twas nobly done, O Herndon!
   And thy name shall ever be
In manhood's lexicon a word
   Expressing chivalry.
Well may the Old Dominion,
   Who gave us Washington,
And many other noble names,
   Be proud of such a son.

With placid brow the brave man saw
   The helpless ones depart,
And then a heavy load of care
   Seemed lifted from his heart.
He viewed them as they left the ship
   Tossed on the billows wild,

Then from his lip the sentence broke,
"God help *my* wife and child!"

When the ill-fated ship went down,
  Of all that luckless band
Alone her brave commander stood,
  A rocket in his hand.
To the last gasp he clung to her,
  And then, the struggle o'er,
He calmly closed his eyes in death,
  And sank to rise no more.

Calm be thy rest, O noble heart!
  Upon thy ocean bed;
Than thine there is no worthier name
  Among the gallant dead.
Thy fate was mournful, but the world
  Shall speak thy virtues rare,
While God-like truth exists, and men
  Are brave and women fair.

PEACE, BE STILL!

Like a vast caldron seemed the sea!
   On sped the gallant bark!
Like a caged ocean bird set free
   Upon the waters dark.
Shrieking, the storm-fiend hurried by,
   Speaking of woe and wreck;
But 'bove his voice arose the cry,
   "We perish, Lord, awake!"

O wondrous change! O heavenly balm!
   Borne on the storm-filled air,
A sweet, low voice, fell like a charm
   Upon each ravished ear.
It was the Master—"Peace, be still!"
   He said, and the mad sea

At once, in answer to his will,
   Was all tranquillity.

How sweet the thought when dangers crowd
   Around us to appall,
That with firm trust we may aloud
   Upon the Saviour call!
How sweet the faith that makes all bright
   And leads us gently home,
Where dangers can no more affright,
   And sorrow can not come.

WORLD-WEARY.

Weary, weary, oh! how weary
   Is she of the cold world's strife!
Dreary, dreary, oh! how dreary
   Is the path of her sad life!
Grim the phantoms that pursue her
   Ever, ever, night and day!
Whispering dark words unto her,
   Chasing hope and faith away.

Not a trusted friend is near her,
   In the world she stands alone;
None to soothe her, none to cheer her,
   Wronged, uncared for, and unknown.
Gazes she upon the water,
   Dazed her brain and wild her eye,

Breathes the prayer her mother taught her,
　And then plunges in to die!

Rash the deed, but judge her kindly
　Ye who gaze on horrified!
Had she never loved so blindly,
　She would never thus have died.
Raise her form, all bruised and broken,
　Lay it gently 'neath the sod;
Let not one harsh word be spoken,
　Leave her failings all with God.

THE BEGGAR-GIRL'S COMPLAINT.

"Old Santa Claus has come again!"
   The rich man's children cry,
And health glows in their ruddy cheeks
   As they run shouting by.
I do not envy them their toys,
   Nor would I check their glee;
But oh! I wish that Santa Claus
   Would visit Sue and me!

They say he's merry, kind, and free;
   But I am very sure,
Though this may be his character,
   He does not like the poor.
For if he did, he'd call on them,
   And give them of his store,

Instead of striding coldly on
    Past every poor man's door.

I do not want his pretty toys,
    His candies or his fruits;
I'd rather have, by far, a frock
    Or pair of winter boots,
Or a nice warm stove to sit by,
    Or a bonnet for the street,
Or a pair of woolen stockings,
    Or a loaf of bread to eat.

Oh! if *I* were old Santa Claus,
    I know what I would do;
I'd visit rich men's houses,
    But I'd visit poor homes too.
And if I blessed the rich man's child
    With toys and dainties sweet,
I'd give the poor warm clothes to wear,
    And food enough to eat.

I'd go to every lonely hut,
   And every palace grand,
And scatter presents everywhere
   With an unsparing hand.
And Christmas morning, when the bells
   Gave out a joyful sound,
Not one sad face or bleeding heart
   Should in the world be found.

Oh! if I were old Santa Claus,
   I'd make all sad homes bright;
Boys should not swear, and lie, and steal;
   Nor parents drink and fight;
Nor should poor homeless wanderers
   Be treated cruelly,
While plodding through the bleak, dark streets,
   Like little Sue and me.

But I am not old Santa Claus;
   I'm but a beggar-girl,

Who's buffeted and kicked about,
    In the great city's whirl.
Not one kind voice addresses me,
    None heed the pangs I feel,
And so to keep myself alive
    I have to beg and steal.

O men! who b'lieve that Christ the **Lord**
    Was poor while on the earth,
Steel not your hearts against us
    On the morning of his birth;
But as your well-clad little ones
    Throng round you in their glee,
Give one kind thought to such poor waifs
    As little Sue and me.

ELSIE'S DEATH.

"Out of the mouths of babes and sucklings hast Thou ordained strength."—Psalm 8 : 2.

An infant form lay stark and cold,
   In its last sad habit drest,
But the smile on its angel features told
   How calm it had sunk to rest.
And tears down its mother's pale cheek rolled,
As she kissed her darling, stark and cold.

A little girl—the dead one's twin—
   Stood gazing on the scene;
She nothing knew of death or sin,
   And wondered what could mean
Her mother's lamentations loud
While o'er her darling's corse she bowed.

"What ails my little sister dear?
　Sweet mamma, tell me, pray.
I've watched her lying silent here
　Throughout the livelong day.
She does not seem to feel or hear—
What ails my sister, mamma dear?"

"She's dead, my child; your sister's dead—
　She can not play again;
Her spirit has forever fled
　From grief, and sin, and pain.
And yet, O God! my heart will break
When my last look at her I take!"

"Mamma, have you not often said
　That when good people die,
They go where no more tears are shed—
　With God, beyond the sky?
I love my sister, mamma dear,
But would not, could I, keep her here.

"For Elsie, I am sure, is there—
　So, mamma, let *us* die;
And to her in that home so fair
　Together let us fly!
I'm very sure, mamma, that *she*
　Is watching now for you and me!"

"I thank thee, God!" the mother cried,
　"Now I can bear my loss.
Come, kneel, sweet one, with me beside
　Your little sister's corse;
Raise up your hands, my precious one,
And pray, 'Thy will, not mine, be done!'"

THE OLD KNICKERBOCKER'S SONG.

Give me the good old days again,
When hearts were true and manners plain;
When boys were boys till fully grown,
And baby belles were never known;
When doctors' bills were light and few,
And lawyers had not much to do;
When honest toil was well repaid,
And theft had not become a trade.

Give me the good old days again,
When cider was not called champagne,
And round the fire in wintry weather,
Nuts and dry jokes were cracked together;
When girls their lovers battled for
With seeds from juicy apple's core,

While mam and dad looked on with glee,
Well pleased their merriment to see.

Give me the good old days again,
When only healthy stock was slain;
When flour was pure, and milk was sweet,
And sausages were fit to eat;
When children early went to bed,
And ate no sugar on their bread;
When lard was not turned into butter,
And tradesmen only truth would utter.

Give me the good old days again,
When women were not proud and vain;
When fashion did not sense outrun,
And tailors had no need to dun;
When wealthy parents were not fools,
And common sense was taught in schools;
When hearts were warm and friends were true,
And Satan had not much to do.

The Old Knickerbocker's Song.

Give me the good old days again,
Ere fraud and violence had reign;
When voters did not look for booty,
And judges dared to do their duty.
When patriots were not bought and sold,
But worked for country—not for gold;
When every citizen could vote
Without a dagger at his throat.

Give me the good old days again,
When our exchequer felt no drain;
When men in place, to "grind their axes,"
Swelled not our public debts and taxes.
When alms-house keepers had some feeling,
And lived in clover without stealing.
Alas! alas! I sigh in vain
To see those good old days again.

THE FIREMAN'S DEATH.

He slept, and o'er his dauntless brow a shade of sorrow stole,
As though some scene of deep distress was busy with his soul,
When suddenly the dread alarm came ringing shrill and clear,
Cleaving the night air till it struck upon his startled ear.

    He bounded up! His practiced eye
    Was turned upon the lurid sky,
    Lit by the flames which, mounting higher,
    Soon clothed the night in a robe of fire.

With lightning speed he reached the scene—oh! what a sight was there!
A mother stood amid the flames, and shrieked in wild despair!

Her arms around her frightened babe were
    thrown with frenzied clasp,
As though she feared the fire-fiend would tear it
    from her grasp.
  With helmet turned, through flame and smoke
  The gallant fellow fearless broke;
  He saved them both, but ah! his life
  Was lost in the unequal strife.

Now in sweet Greenwood's peaceful shade the
    noble hero sleeps,
And o'er his grave full many a friend in silent
    sorrow weeps,
A monument erected there is pointed to with
    pride
By those with whom he oft has fought the fire,
    side by side.
  Sweet flowers exhale their fragrant breath
  Where now he calmly sleeps in death,
  And trees their spreading branches wave
  Around his solemn Greenwood grave.

LINES

ON THE DEATH OF A YOUNG LADY WHO DIED ONLY FOUR WEEKS AFTER MARRIAGE.

Proudly stood they at the altar,
    Loving friends on every side—
He a young and joyous bridegroom,
    She a youthful, blushing bride.
Pure her soul as were the flowers
    That enwreathed her virgin brow—
Passed she like a vision from us,
    And she is an angel now.

Four short weeks a bride was Carrie,
    Full of wedded happiness,
Then we laid her down to slumber
    In her pure white bridal dress.

Brilliant was she in her beauty,
   As she took her nuptial vow,
But she was too pure for earth-life,
   And she is an angel now.

Jesus wept o'er the departed—
   Even he felt mortal woe—
And when loved ones vanish from us,
   Hearts *will* ache and tears will flow.
Weep then, friends, and stricken husband;
   But in meek submission bow
To the will of God—for, surely,
   Carrie is an angel now.

RELIGION.

Hail, blest Religion! safeguard of the free!
Destroyer of foul vice, mother of purity,
Thou white-robed seraph at whom skeptics rail—
Balm of the bleeding heart, Religion, hail!
Many profess to own thy sacred flame,
And day by day invoke thy blessed name
In gorgeous temples, built with jealous care;
But let's look in and see if thou art there.

See, in yon cushioned pew, with downcast look,
A man sits poring o'er a well-thumbed book;
All richly dressed is he in vestments rare;
And as the holy man pours forth his prayer
His face assumes a penitential air,
Mingled *somewhat*, methinks, with worldly care.

Now his pale countenance betokens pain,
And tears are falling from his eyes like rain!
He reads a memorandum book of loss and gain!
Its contents have convinced him, plain as day,
That some of his dear cash has flown away.
He whispers *her* his loss, and, musing on it,
His wife is grieving for her next new bonnet.

In a darksome corner, almost hid from view,
Sits one who has the aspect of a Jew.
He's dozing now, and now begins to nod,
And, sleeping holds communion with *his* god,
His gilded god: that man his daughter sold—
His only daughter—for a heap of gold.

Now cast your eye on yonder youthful pair,
Who seem Devotion's counterpart—how fair
And pure they look, those lovely girls!
List! their religion's centered in their curls!

"My gracious, Emma! look at Martha's hair!
How illy it's arranged, I declare!"

But turn we round our eyes, and gaze we now
Upon a *Christian*, whose unclouded brow
Speaks the tranquillity that reigns within
His breast. He is not free from sin—
(None are, though some pretend to be,
And elongate their faces piously;
They never smile—not they—they'd sooner cry,
And agonize and groan, and sweat and sigh.)
He believes that every creature born of woman
Has passions, and "to step aside is human."
He toiling earns his bread—does all he can
To be what God intended him—a man.

'Twould fill a book to mention every one—
The luckless debtor and the heartless dun;
The widow poor, who scarce her bread can
    earn,

Rising from prayer to meet the landlord stern;
The beggar, perishing through lack of food,
Doubting the policy of doing good,
And, losing every thought of future weal,
Goes forth from prayer constrained almost to steal.

Yes, visit any city church—you'll find
Within its walls all grades of human kind;
But underneath the peasant's humble roof
(From which the rich man sneering stands aloof)
The "peace which passeth understanding" lives—
That priceless peace which *true* Religion gives.
There Nature works, and from the emerald sod
Around the poor man's cottage, up to God
The flowers their incense breathe, as if in prayer;
And every bird that carols in the air,
And every breeze that sweeps the forest wild,
Speaks of Religion, "pure and undefiled."

RAT, THE NEWSBOY,

ON THE LATE FRIGHTFUL ACCIDENT.

My name is Jimmy Connors, which they calls me Rat, for short—
I'm fourteen, weigh a hundred pounds, likewise I'm fond of sport.
I'm a newsboy, and a bootblack, and I carry bundles too—
In fact, I tackle any job that I am fit to do.

You ask about the accident that happened at the ferry—
I'd rather talk of something else—it makes me feel bad—very.

I can't drive it from my mind, sir, oh! it was
 a fearful sight.
I'm thinking of it all day long and dream of
 it at night.

But as you seem to wish it, I'll tackle it once
 more,
And tell you, near as possible, exactly what I
 saw.
'Twas Sunday, as you know, sir, and nearly one
 o'clock,
And I was with my brother, a-fishin' on the
 dock.

We hadn't been a-sittin' on the stone pier very
 long,
When suddintly we heard the sound of steam
 a-blowin' strong,

And then there came a rumblin' noise, and then a crash—a snorter!
And then my brother lost his seat and tumbled in the water.

I was dizzy for a minnit, so suddint was the shock,
And then I stirred myself to help my brother on the dock.
I roared to see him crawlin' out, and then I fell to chaffin';
But in a minit more, you bet, I didn't feel like laffin'.

Quicker'n I can tell it, there came a rush o' steam,
But 'bove the noise it made I heard a hundred people scream;

My hair riz up, my blood ran cold, so orful did it sound,
And then a crowd of drownin' folks were strugglin' all around!

It wasn't long before I saw two babies by me float,
And then, like winkin', I threw off my shoes, and vest, and coat,
And plungin' in, I swam to 'em, and brought 'em safe ashore;
And then I hurried back agin, to try and save some more.

I came near blubberin', you bet, but 'twas no time for cryin'
When men and women, boys and girls, were all around us dyin';

And so I labored with a will till I was tired out,
And then I stopped awhile to rest myself and look about.

And such a sight I hope, sir, I shall never see again!
Some dead and others dying—some ravin' mad with pain!
The air was full of screams, and oaths, and prayers, and sighs, and groans—
Some had no arms nor legs—some had the flesh torn from their bones!

I rested but a minit when I went to work again,
For lookin' at such sights, you bet, went rather 'gainst the grain.

I'm nothin' but a boy, sir, but I did the best
  I could;
If I had been a man, I think I might ha' did
  some good.*

And now, in few words as I could I've told
  you all I saw.
And so, not wishin' to offend, I think I'll chin
  no more;
I'm onto bissiness now, you see, for it is after
  nine—
Your boots is very dirty, sir—say, won't you
  take a shine?

---

* It is estimated that "Rat" saved at least ten persons.

WHAT ARE THE SAD WAVES SAYING?

WHAT are the sad waves saying
Evermore,
As they in ceaseless playing
Kiss the shore?
They are saying,
In their swaying,
O'er and o'er:
"On the shore we're dying—
Time is onward flying—
And life's waves are rolling
Beyond man's controlling
Evermore!"

What are the sad waves saying
Evermore,

What are the sad Waves saying?

As they in ceaseless playing
   Kiss the shore?
They are saying,
In their swaying,
   O'er and o'er:
"Joy has no to-morrow,
Life is full of sorrow,
And the restless ocean
Types the soul's commotion
   Evermore."

What are the sad waves saying
   Evermore,
As they in ceaseless playing
   Kiss the shore?
They are saying,
In their swaying,
   O'er and o'er:
"O ye lovers walking,
Fondly, sweetly talking

On the strand,
Fervent vows, rose-tinted,
Are like lines imprinted
On the sand."

What are the sad waves saying
Evermore,
As they in ceaseless playing
Kiss the shore?
They are saying,
In their swaying,
O'er and o'er:
" Foolish boy or maiden,
Dreaming of sweet Aiden
On the shore,
Time will prove your treasures
And your keenest pleasures
Day-dreams—nothing more!"

TO THE BABY.

Crow, kick, and stretch, baby!
Though crowing be a *fowl* offense,
It can not touch thy innocence;
And though thy tiny, unskilled ear,
Like that of noisy chanticleer,
No knowledge hath of time or tune
At present, it will alter soon,
And you may try a higher strain;
But till such time I say again,
Crow, kick, and stretch, baby!

Crow, kick, and stretch, baby!
Though kicking may not be genteel
Except in polka, jig, or reel,
Thou canst not yet essay to dance
The latest hop brought o'er from France;

And so thy feet should privileged be
To kick the air right merrily.
Till thou hast learned the power of song,
And thy young limbs are lithe and strong,
 Crow, kick, and stretch, baby!

 Crow, kick, and stretch, baby!
Stretching was e'er the wisest plan
For helpless babe or grown-up man.
Man, shrinking 'neath the frown of care,
Should stretch to keep his head in air,
And babe, if he would thrive and grow,
Should stretch himself from top to toe.
Then till the difference 'twixt the two
You learn, I'll tell thee what to do—
 Crow, kick, and stretch, baby!

LIFE AND DEATH.

How beautiful is life in its bright morning,
   Ere the heart knoweth aught of care or woe,
Or the pure soul has felt the first sad warning
   That sin envelopeth all things below!

How beautiful is life when, crowned with roses,
   Fond youth by turns rejoices, sighs, and loves,
Or in an ideal bower of bliss reposes,
   Or through the sunny vales of fancy roves.

How beautiful is life, though proud ambition
   Shuts out the light of childhood's happy years!
Man, striving hard to better his condition,
   Forgets the while his misery and tears.

How beautiful is life, e'en when advances
   Old age to bend the frame and dim the eye!
The tottering pilgrim backward ever glances,
   And never, never is prepared to die.

But, oh! to me how vapid seems this yearning
   To cling to earth with all its woe and pain.
What is there here to quench this inward burn-
   ing?
What is there on this sordid earth to gain?

How beautiful is death! How calm and quiet
   The features are, fixed in its sweet repose.
The pulseless heart—no sorrow now can try it—
   'Tis freed forever from all earthly woes.

How beautiful is death! That form so lately
   Racked by sharp pain and agonized by fear,
Now wears a look serenely grand and stately,
   While lying silent on its sombre bier.

How beautiful is death! All strife is ended,
   Nor can ambition, pride, nor black despair,
Nor any other ill that life attended,
   Lay its rude, caustic, envious finger there.

O life and death! ye puzzles to vain mortals,
   And both so fair, viewed by philosophy,
Shall we, when past the gloomy grave's dark portals,
   Rend the thick vail that hides the mystery?

SPOIL THE ROD AND SPARE THE CHILD.

MEN and women, Shakespeare tells us,
   Are but children larger grown;
This is true as truth can make it—
   Few are fit to run alone.
Not an adult soul among us
   But some folly has beguiled;
Then when little ones are faulty,
   Spoil the rod and spare the child.

Anger only wakens anger—
   Love it is that rules the heart;
Force restrains, but does not conquer,
   Though the bitter tear may start.
If you'd reach an erring bosom,
   Trust to reason and be mild,

Give not way to brutal passion—
   Spoil the rod and spare the child.

.

If, with all his boasted knowledge,
   Man is changeable and weak,
Can he, with a show of reason,
   Perfectness in childhood seek?
Oh! then gently deal with children,
   If they wayward prove and wild,
Love will bring them to submission—
   Spoil the rod and spare the child.

Never yet did boy of spirit
   Feel the sharp lash to his gain;
If by love you can not rule him,
   You may lacerate in vain.
Glorious, bright-eyed, romping childhood
   By each harsh blow is defiled;
Oh! then treat the darlings gently—
   Spoil the rod and spare the child.

BE KIND TO YOUR MOTHER.

Be kind to your mother! Oh! be not ungrateful
  When age dims her eye, or disease racks her frame;
No fault in mankind shows more glaring and hateful,
  Than that which would lead us her foibles to blame.
She has borne with our follies in life's early stage,
And should we not, then, bear with hers in her age?

Be kind to your mother! Has she not stood near you
  When loathsome disease caused all others to fly?
To comfort, to solace, to nurse, and to cheer you—
  Yes, even if called on, to suffer and die?
Then in her decline you should never demur,
If you have to labor and suffer for her.

Be kind to your mother! Be duteous and grateful—
  The heart's deepest rev'rence and love are her due;
And if of these natural claims you're neglectful,
  Look not for respect from your children to you.
Each unfilial action against you is scored,
And when you grow old, you will reap your reward.

Be kind to your mother; for fast she is failing,
  And soon she will sink 'neath the sad weight of years,
And all your regrets will then prove unavailing—
  Your actions can not be erased by your tears.
Then guard well your passions, be patient and mild—
'Tis the least that a mother expects from her child.

WHY ART THOU COLD?

(DESIGNED FOR MUSIC.)

Why art thou cold and careless while I'm near thee?
  Has thy vain heart proved recreant to me?
Dost thou seek other eyes and lips to cheer thee?
  And art thou really anxious to be free?
With all my soul, then let us kiss and sever,
  I would not hold thee captive 'gainst thy will.
O thou once wildly loved! farewell forever,
  Thy voice will ne'er again my pulses thrill.

Thou art false to me—another kneels before thee
  To whisper love in thy too willing ear.
To swear that he forever will adore thee—
  I hope for thy sake that he is sincere.

As for myself, I'm willing he should woo thee,
  I'm willing thou shouldst call him all thine own,
I would not whisper one objection to thee;
  I love thee not, my heart has callous grown.

'Tis vain to say that love, though scorned and slighted
  Day after day, will suffer and live on;
By cold neglect the fondest love is blighted,
  It lives not when its aliment is gone.
I loved thee once, and would have loved forever,
  Hadst thou been true and loyal unto me;
The spell is broken—thou art free, and never
  Shall my proud heart deplore the loss of thee

TO MY SISTER IN CALIFORNIA.

Thou art far away, my sister,
   And we miss thee when we meet
Together, as when thou wert here,
   To hold communion sweet;
We miss thee, and *another one*—
   Two seats are vacant now,
For one has had the seal of death
   Stamped on her angel brow.

Two months ago, two little months,
   The music of her voice
Would make the dullest eye light up,
   The saddest heart rejoice;
But now 'tis hushed for aye in death,
   Her frame lies 'neath the sod,

And her sweet voice has joined the choir
  Around the throne of God.

And our dear mother! oh! how well
  She bears the heavy blow:
A heavenly, calm serenity
  Seems mingled with her woe;
She merely says, "So pass away
  My children, one by one;
Still, I must humbly kiss the rod—
  Father, thy will be done!"

O darling sister! how my soul
  Is melted into tears,
As memory takes me back again
  To those thrice happy years
When *all* our flock were gathered round
  Our happy, cheerful hearth,
And not a care was mingled with
  Our ever-rising mirth.

Now some are dead, and some, like you,
    Have wandered far away,
And we have only memory's voice
    To cheer us, day by day;
Yet still we hug the darling hope—
    God grant it be not vain!
That we shall one day hail the strayed
    Around our hearth again.

Oh! well do I remember now
    Your every word and look
When, bowed in silent agony,
    Our last farewell we took;
My quivering lip and stammering tongue
    No solace could impart,
For oh! a fearful storm of grief
    Was swelling in my heart.

Then every loving word of thine,
    And every action kind,

With ten-fold force came thronging back
  Upon my anguished mind.
As memory clings to joys that fly
  And leave the heart forlorn,
So those we love while at our side
  Seem dearer when they're gone.

Best, kindest sister, years may roll
  Ere we again can meet,
But thou art in my heart of hearts,
  While memory holds her seat!
Speed swiftly, time, increase thy pace
  Till the last hour has flown
That keeps my sister's anxious breast
  From throbbing 'gainst my own.

CARRIERS' ADDRESS.

NEW-YORK, JANUARY 1, 1854.

TIME has been called "the cheat of human bliss,"
Still we must all, I think, agree in this—
That though remorseless in his swift career,
He bids us all be happy once a year.
And so all might, were't not that grief may stand
Beside the "cheat" with hour-glass in hand,
And throw o'er some of us a shade of woe
To check our joyous spirits' mirthful flow.
Thus many, since the birth of '53
Was ushered in by mirth and minstrelsy,
Have by affliction's hand been made to feel
A wound that time may strive in vain to heal.

In '53 round many a social hearth,
Where happy hearts indulged in noisy mirth,
May now be seen the sad and silent room,
The scene of apathy and sombre gloom.
Instead of mirth-strains, tears unbidden rise
To dim the lustre of once joy-lit eyes.
A seat is vacant—one loved form is gone—
A bud from off the parent stem is torn—
One chord is snapt upon the golden lute—
The charm is broken—all the rest are mute.

But how is this? Egad! we must confess
We're getting over-grave in our address!
Ye shades of woe,.perplex us not. Away!
Pray, what have we to do with you to-day?
Avaunt, ye monsters! off! begone! take wings!
And let us speak awhile of happier things:
Of sweet reunions and heart-thrilling eyes;
Of well-cooked poultry and smoking pies;

Of friends, long absent, met—of truthful hearts;
Of puddings, pastry, condiments, and tarts;
Of happy little folks with lots of toys,
And happy big folks, making lots of noise;
Of ladies booking imaginary "calls;"
Of parties, concerts, theatres, and balls;
Of old men talking o'er their youthful tricks,
And young men ("fast" ones) "going it, like bricks."
And—let us see—it is in part our charge
To say a word about the world at large.

<blockquote>
Of England much can not be said.
She still preserves her mighty trade,
And still can boast the truest Queen
That ever on her throne has been,
One who, howe'er the nation fares,
Will keep it well supplied with heirs,
And who, a monarch though she be,
Finds time to tend her family.
</blockquote>

Oh! that her lords and commons would
Something enact for Erin's good—
Something to stop the blight that runs
Like lightning 'mid her famished sons!
The Dublin Crystal Palace dome
Looks down upon how many a home
Where haggard want and fell despair
A nation's misery declare!
Within the walls of brilliant glass
The wealth of labor, but alas!
Without the walls, on Erin's soil,
Is famishing the son of toil!
Enough of this. 'Tis now our wish
To turn from Ireland to fish,
(A scaly subject, and not new,
Though one of some importance too.)
For many years the north-west coast
Was thronged each season by a host
Of stalwart fishers, bronzed and brave,
Who made their living on the wave.

So far, so good. One day, John Bull,
Of beer, roast beef, and wisdom full,
Discovered that they had no right
To fish. He was mistaken quite;
For Jonathan, to John Bull's wonder,
Sent out a force to keep him under;
And while they talk the matter o'er,
We keep on fishing, as before.
There have been some unimportant other
Disputes between the child and mother,
But still there is not like to be
Any real cause for enmity.

Proud France still owns the third Napoleon's sway—
At least, we heard she did, the other day.
How soon the steamer may bring other news—
A total change of rulers and of views,

My "uncle's nephew" to grim Pluto sent,
The election of another President,
The restoration of the Bourbon crown,
'Mid fire, and flame, and pillage, and sacked town;
How soon such stirring news may come this way,
Of course we can not undertake to say—
There's no appearance of such matters now,
But France is quick at getting up a row.

Spain, as of old, imbecile, vain, and proud,
Still puts on airs, looks haughty, and talks loud;
Treats Uncle Sam with evident disdain;
Threatens his children with garrote and chain.
By turns she curses, prays, exhorts, and blusters,
Both at our senators and fillibusters;

She feels our power, is conscious of her weakness,
And of our magnanimity and meekness.

But let us now prepare a sort of lunch—
Put all affairs of moment in a bunch,
Shake them all up without regard to skill,
And let the items come out as they will.

Koszta is here, and relates without fear
How the generous, brave Ingraham got him clear,
    Through Turkish neutrality,
    From Austrian brutality—
An act which will render the captain most dear
In ev'ry free port he may happen to steer.

"The turbulent and turbaned Turk"
    For Nicholas has cut out work,
    And now the bear's in such a stew
    He really knows not what to do.

'Twas he commenced the row, and so
He can not well "back down," you know,
Without a loss of power and pride
That every nation would deride.
His bearship could afford to dance,
But for old Albion and France;
Though they are in the way, and so
The Czar's face wears a look of woe.

Now, here's a piece of glorious news:
A war among the famed "foo-foos"
Has broken out; the Chinese now,
We trust, will shortly cease to bow
The willing knee to senseless "Josh,"
When they discover 'tis all "bosh;"
And thus an opening will be made
For Christian folks to push new trade.
Besides, we have a work began
With jealous-minded, close Japan,

Whose Emperor has talked with Perry,
And treated him politely—very.

We've got to settle with Peru
For maltreating a Yankee crew.
For such act no offense we gave her,
And her guano will not save her,
Unless she promises that she
Will never more pugnacious be.

Science and art still do their part
  To keep mankind in motion,
The march of mind we yet may find
  On land and on the ocean:
Machines infernal, improvements internal,
  Roads, sewers, and canals,
Fat cattle and hogs, fast horses and dogs,
  Fine boys and "bouncing gals;"
Soon we'll let slip from "Mississippi"
  An iron-horse terrific,

To whisk us all, both great and small,
    From this to the Pacific.

The fabrics rare in our World's Fair
    Show that we've not been sleeping;
Industry here, 'tis very clear,
    A harvest rich is reaping.
"Vic's" house of glass may ours surpass
    In size, but not in beauty;
With plastic hands our artisans
    Have nobly done their duty.

To this free shore are flocking o'er
    The oppressed of every nation,
Who here may sup from freedom's cup,
    Unfearing molestation.
Mitchel and Meagher everywhere
    Have met a cordial greeting,
And *all* we heed, whate'er their creed,
    If freedom prompts their meeting.

From California still arrives
  "Hull heaps" of golden ore,
And reckless miners hold their lives
  As cheaply as before.
Not satisfied with all the wealth
  The gold land has before her,
They've struck their tents and took by stealth
  A new field in Sonora.
Just think of it! in less time than
  A "grizzly" would a cub lick,
Walker on Mexico "shut pan,"
  And formed a new republic.

There! we have done.
May every one—
  Boys, girls, men, maids, and matrons;
The short, the tall,
Each one and all,
  Who call themselves our patrons—

Be glad to-day,
Happy and gay,
   And may no cloud of sorrow
Arise to mar
Life's brilliant star
   On any future morrow.
May every comfort wealth can bring,
Every song that joy can sing,
Every pleasure without a sting—
In short, each dearly-cherished thing—
   A magic spell
Weave round you while time's on the wing,
   And so farewell:
But do not forget, as mirth takes you along,
You've been reading the carrier's annual song.

ALONE AMONG THE SHADOWS.

I'm alone among the shadows,
   And I'm waiting for the light,
To chase away the visions
   Of the dreary, weary night.
Like a sightless child deserted
   My uncertain way I grope—
I'm alone among the shadows,
   But my soul is full of hope.

I'm alone among the shadows;
   But my doubts and fears are past,
For I feel the sweet assurance
   That the light will come at last.

A ray from hope's bright beacon
    Comes through the gloom to me—
I'm alone among the shadows,
    But my heart is light and free.

I'm alone among the shadows;
    But I hear a sweet voice say,
"You would not prize the daylight
    If it were always day."
And so I'll strive in earnest
    To keep from error free,
And He who strengtheneth the weak
    Will surely comfort me.

TO HATE.

Thou baleful, black-browed, murderous thing!
    Thou bane of human bliss!
Thou vampire fiend of sombre wing,
    Whose loathsome, lep'rous kiss
Blisters the lips it meets, and turns
    Life's sweets to bitterest gall,
And like a hungry fire burns
    In souls that own thy thrall.

Thank God, I ne'er have known thee yet,
    Vile monster that thou art!
Thou ne'er hast had and ne'er can get
    A lodgment in my heart.

Though I were doomed to feel the sting
    Of enmity's foul blow,
I'd seek no shelter 'neath thy wing,
    Thou minister of woe.

I can afford to pity thee,
    And all whose guide thou art;
For no poor wretch from pain is free
    While thou dost rule his heart.
I'd rather suffer from thy spite
    Than own thee as my friend;
For love, thy master, will delight
    When thou hast reached thine end.

HERE'S A HEALTH TO THOSE WHO LOVE US.

Here's a health to those who love us,
   And a smile for those who hate;
Kind heaven is above us,
   And we may trust our fate.
If loved ones fly before us,
   And those who hate, betray,
God's mercy still is o'er us
   On sorrow's darkest day.
Then a health to those who love us,
   And a smile for those who hate,
Kind heaven is above us,
   And we may trust our fate.

The love that in an hour
   Will plume its wings and fly
Elsewhere to try its power,
   Is hardly worth a sigh.

The hate that would annoy us
  Is only worth a smile;
It never can destroy us,
  For heaven rules the while.
Then a health to those who love us,
  And a smile for those who hate;
Kind heaven is above us,
  And we may trust our fate.

This life is but a bubble,
  'Tis ended in a day;
Then let us laugh at trouble,
  And drive our cares away.
The world is full of sorrow,
  But has its pleasures too;
Then do not trouble borrow,
  Life's bright side only view.
Then a health to those who love us,
  And a smile for those who hate;
Kind heaven is above us,
  And we may trust our fate.

HE'S TEN YEARS OLD TO-DAY.

Look at him as he bounds along!
  The red-cheeked, bright-eyed boy!
His well-knit limbs so lithe and strong,
  His shout so full of joy!
School's not in yet—he's full of glee,
  And ripe for any play;
His little heart is full, for he
  Is ten years old to-day.

His roomy pockets plethoric
  With top, and cord, and ball,
And rags, and stones, and bits of stick,
  And other trifles small.
The hour is his, his mind is free,
  So get not in his way—

Is he not rich? besides, you see,
  He's ten years old to-day.

He is a prince among the boys
  On this his natal morn;
Above them all you hear his voice,
  Clear as a bugle-horn.
He laughs, he screams, he runs "like mad,"
  No colt could wilder play—
But prythee do not scold the lad,
  He's ten years old to-day.

O happy boy! so free from care,
  How sad it is to know
That time will mark thy forehead fair
  With trouble, toil, and woe!
But, haply, you're untrammeled now,
  So frolic while you may—
Though grief at last may shade thy brow
  You're only ten to-day.

ALL BORN IN OCTOBER.

AFFECTIONATELY INSCRIBED TO F. S. STREET.

Father, mother, and children three,
All members of one family,
A curious thing indeed to see—
    All born in sad October.

No birthday record do they need;
If they the year and day but heed,
The month is very plain indeed—
    For each it is October.

All came when leaves were brown and sere,
And nature's face was dark and drear,
The saddest season of the year—
    The month of brown October.

But may no envious autumn come
To cast a shadow on their home,
And may their lives be sunshine from
    October to October.

Around the white throne may they stand,
A still united, happy band,
When they have reached the "better land,"
    Where there is no October.

Father, mother, and children three,
All members of one family,
A curious thing indeed to see—
    All born in sad October.

HARD LUCK.

I took my place the other day
   On board a ferry-boat,
And looked around, as is my wont,
   The passengers to note.
Two young mechanics going home
   From work were standing near,
Whose colloquy I listened to,
   And will repeat it here.

"O Jack!" said one, "the other day
   I fell against Tom Duff,
And I tell you I pitied him,
   He looked so awful rough.
His toggery was all in rags,
   No shoes were on his feet,

In fact, he looked as hard a case
    As any on the street.

"I asked about his family.
    His wife, he said, was dead,
And his two little children
    Were suffering for bread.
He'd had no work for nigh a month,
    And gone was all his pluck;
He never could succeed, because
    He'd had such horrid luck."

Jack listened to his friend's report,
    And then he heaved a sigh,
And then he said, "I pity Tom; but Bob,
    'Twixt you and I,
This horrid luck we hear about,
    Unless I am mistaken,
Instead of being sent to us
    Is often of our makin'.

"Now, Tom and I were 'prentice boys
    Together, as you know,
And he was very quick to learn,
    While I was very slow.
He always could earn more than me,
    And dressed like any buck;
But he could never keep a cent,
    He had such awful luck.

"He had no one to work for—
    His wages, every cent,
Were his—while I was forced to pay
    My widowed mother's rent.
And yet so awful was his luck,
    He never had a dime,
And he has borrowed stamps from me
    To get beer many a time.

"Both of us married early,
    And both got thrifty wives;

There should have been no difference
   In the current of our lives.
If any thing, my expenses
   Were the greatest; for you see
While Tom has but two little ones,
   Kind heaven has sent me three.

"Tom's wife was young and beautiful,
   But wasn't very strong,
And being obliged to work so hard,
   She couldn't stand it long.
She never ventured out of doors,
   But to her babies stuck,
While Tom sat in some drinking-shop
   A-growling at his luck.

"Now, I've no reason to complain,
   I'm doing very well;
Sometimes indeed when work gives out
   I have an idle spell;

But then I always try to keep
    A stamp or two ahead,
And never yet have had to hear
    My babies cry for bread.

"I'm just as sorry for poor Tom
    As you can be, friend Jack,
And I would rather help him on
    Than try to set him back.
But I have always noticed
    When a fellow guzzles rum,
And loafs about and takes his ease,
    Hard luck is sure to come."

THE WILLOW.

I LOVE the lofty poplar
   And the tall, majestic pine,
I love the sturdy oak, round which
   The creeping ivies twine.
I love the generous trees that yield
   Kind nature's bounteous store,
But, though it has a mournful look,
   I love the willow more.

'Tis not because the cares of life
   Have steeped my soul in woe
That I dearly love to gaze upon
   Its branches waving low.
No, 'tis not that; for while I gaze
   It calls up to my view

The sweetest, brightest, gayest hours
  My boyhood ever knew.

'Twas underneath a willow tree,
  Beside a running stream,
Where I in childhood, tired out,
  Had many a sweet day-dream
About dear Minnie Morrison,
  Who often played with me,
And whose bright face and sunny curls
  I even now can see.

O glorious Minnie Morrison!
  Full thirty years have fled
Since then, and you, perhaps, may now
  Be sleeping with the dead.
But if you still are on the earth,
  Wherever you may be,
I know that in your reveries
  You sometimes think of me.

O willow! dear old willow,
  Where are the friends who played
With me in happy childhood
  Beneath thy cooling shade?
Some dead, and some have wandered,
  Some remember me no more,
But thou hast still the same kind look
  That greeted me of yore.

MEAGHER'S ESCAPE.*

There's a voice in the gale, speeding over the waters,
  A song of rejoicing, a burden of glee,
A pean from Erin's brave sons and fair daughters,
  "Old Ireland's defender, young Meagher, is free!"
They could not enslave him; for on her broad pinions
  The Genius of Liberty day after day
Hovered over his head, and from tyranny's minions
  At length bore the noble-souled patriot away.

* First published under a *nom de plume* in 1852.

With honor he shook off the shackles that bound
    him,
  His parole gave up ere he ventured his plan;
And then in broad day, with his enemies round
    him,
    Cried, "Now I defy ye! Take me, if you
      can!"
But vain their endeavors; his steed like a swallow
  Flew over the ground with his rider so brave;
And soon they found out it was useless to follow,
  For Meagher was safely afloat on the wave.

Oh! how must the news of the captive's achieve-
    ment—
  The tidings that he had his liberty won—
Have chased, as the sun does the mist, the be-
    reavement
  Of those who stood round him at Slievena-
    mon!

How eyes must have sparkled and hearts must have bounded,
  And hills must have echoed with cheer upon cheer,
From the wild throbbing bosoms that quickly surrounded
  The bonfire that blazed upon Corrigmoclier!

But it is not his country alone that rejoices;
  The republican host of our own cherished land
In deep exultation are raising their voices,
  And thronging to grasp the young patriot's hand.
"You are welcome," they cry, "to the land of the stranger—
  Thrice welcome beneath our proud eagle's broad wing;
Here safely repose thee, exempt from all danger,
  Protected forever from tyranny's sting.

SHALL WE KNOW THOSE WHO LOVE US?

SHALL we know those who love us,
  When this transient life is o'er,
And we tread the Golden City
  That lies on the other shore?
When we shall reach the spirit-land,
  Will they to us appear
In all their old, familiar guise—
  Just as we knew them here?

When we have cast this mortal off
  For immortality,
And the glad soul, with eager flight,
  Speeds through the ether free,
Will it fly to its blissful home
  Without a taint of earth,

And find its friends assembled there
    To hail the spirit-birth?

Shall we forget our misdeeds
    And our miseries for aye,
And only pleasant memories come,
    Throughout the endless day?
And shall our love, refined and pure,
    Need no chastising rod,
But fill our souls with sweet content,
    And lead us up to God?

O radiant hope! O solace sweet!
    How glorious to be
From all our earth-born phantasies
    For evermore set free!
No longer passion's abject slaves,
    All tribulation o'er—
How sweet to gain a refuge sure
    Where grief can come no more!

THE FELON'S LAST NIGHT.

The felon lay in his gloomy cell,
  His keeper sat close by;
The doomed wretch knew, alas! too well,
  That he must surely die
Before another sun should set;
  And yet how strange that he
Should all his dread of death forget,
  And slumber tranquilly!

He dreamed of childhood's happy hours—
  He heard the robin sing,
And culled again the sweet wild flowers
  That blossomed near the spring;
He saw his mother's look of pride,
  And felt the same sweet joy

As when he frolicked by her side,
  A sinless, happy boy.

Again he lingered on the green,
  And cast his eyes about
In search of little Eveleen,
  When irksome school was out;
Again he saw her sunny smile,
  Her artless, bashful look,
And kissed her rosy cheek the while
  They wandered by the brook.

The sleeper's heart was all aglow
  With innocent delight,
Nor dreamed he that a shade of woe
  Could mar his vision bright;
A sweet smile wreathed his haggard brow;
  A prayer his thin lips moved,
"O Father! thou hast blessed me now—
  I love, and I am loved!"

Ha! what a sound breaks on his ear!
  The solemn prison bell
Rings out the summons loud and clear—
  The prisoner's death-knell!
He springs erect! The look of joy
  Has vanished from his brow!
His dream is o'er; the sinless boy
  Is a doomed felon now!

"Back! back!" he cried, with eyes agleam;
  "Too soon the bell they toll!
I can not die with that sweet dream
  Yet lingering in my soul!
Back! back! Ere ye take me away
  Through yonder prison door,
For Christ's sake grant me leave to stay
  On earth one hour more!"

In vain the felon shrieks aloud,
  And struggles to get free;

They drag him forth before the crowd
    Around the gallows-tree.
The fatal noose is round his neck;
    A priest is standing near,
Beseeching him the cross to take,
    And banish every fear.

A moment's pause. The felon stands
    Like one in dreadful doubt;
Then clinching fast his bony hands,
    Defiantly shrieks out:
"Begone, vile priest! I spit at thee!
    I will not kiss the rod!
I b'lieve not in thy mummery!
    Away! there is no God!

"You say I'm doom'd! Ha! ha! 'tis well!
    No other world I fear—

The Felon's Last Night.

I can not meet a fiercer hell
   Than I have suffered here!"
The cap was drawn, the trap was sprung,
   And on the gallows-tree
The felon's lifeless body swung;
   His soul from earth was free.

WHAT IS LIFE?

To eat, to drink, to strive for fame,
   To lay up heaps of gold;
To pamper self; to toy with shame
   From youth till we are old;
To tread the humdrum round of trade,
   With disappointments rife;
Now filled with hope, and now dismayed,
   Oh! tell me, is this life?

Ah! no; 'tis but the grosser part—
   A fraction of the whole;
The life which satisfies the heart
   Is centred in the soul.
There lie the sanctities that chase
   Away dark error's mist;

That fill us with an inward grace,
   And fit us to exist.

Deep in the soul love rears his throne;
   There truth and faith abide;
And where they rule, ill is unknown,
   And life is glorified.
The outer world, though fair to see,
   Is full of hate and strife;
And oh! how wretched must he be
   Who has no inner life!

THE LASS OF CLOVER LANE.

Sweet are the flowers which bloom around
  The cot where I was born,
And sweet the melody of birds
  That greet the early morn.
Sweet are the daisies and blue-bells
  That gem the verdant plain,
But sweeter than all these to me,
  My lass of Clover lane.

There is no perfume like her breath,
  Nor do the birds excel
The music of her merry laugh,
  Clear as a silver bell,
Pure as a daisy washed with dew—
  As modest, neat and plain—

The queen of love and beauty is
  My lass of Clover Lane.

The city belle whose cheeks are red
  With artificial bloom,
And whose rich gems flash brilliantly
  In ball or concert-room,
May please the pampered man of wealth,
  Conceited, proud, and vain;
But I will pay my homage to
  The lass of Clover Lane.

My darling has no jewels rare,
  Nor can she boast of wealth;
But she is rich in innocence, sweet peace,
  And robust health.
She weeps with those oppressed by woe,
  And at the couch of pain
She is an angel minister,
  My lass of Clover Lane.

So natural, so beautiful,
　So free from guile or art—
Oh! joy to press her to my breast,
　And wear her in my heart.
Should death my angel snatch from me,
　I'd never smile again;
My heart would wither should it lose
　The lass of Clover Lane.

THE HORSE.

Of all the lower animals
  That humbly tread the earth
To work for careless, thankless man,
  The horse has greatest worth.
A very giant in his strength,
  And yet withal so mild,
That he will readily obey
  An invalid or child.

How patient and how tractable,
  How willing he to toil—
A very slave to man, and yet
  The monarch of the soil.
The meanest steed is worth regard,
  But beautiful to see

Is one of choicest lineage
    And perfect symmetry.

No pen can do him justice,
    And e'en the limner's art
Will fail a perfect idea
    Of the racer to impart.
His form may be depicted,
    But the fire in his eye,
The *life* that animates his frame,
    These, every art defy.

Height, sixteen hands—his color, black—
    An arched neck full and strong,
A pair of eyes that shine like stars,
    Mane, tail, and foretop, long.
Ears like a fox's, small and sharp,
    With nostrils large and thin,
And showing, when expanded wide,
    The blood-red tint within.

His haunches moulded splendidly,
    His shoulders large and strong—
Breast full, arms stout, limbs very fine,
    But firm and not too long,
Knees powerful, but clean and trim—
    Hoofs high, with open heels,
Leg action, when in motion, which
    The lightning's speed reveals.

What grace in every movement,
    When his proud blood doth stir!
How he leaps from the solid earth
    In answer to the spur!
He is my equine beau-ideal,
    While bounding o'er the course;
But find him where I may, I love
    The great, strong, noble horse.

COME TO ME, DARLING.

When the red sun in the clear west is glowing,
And the soft wind from the sweet south is blowing,
When the day's trials no longer are near me,
Come to me, darling, to soothe and to cheer me!

Thou art the sun that dispels my sad hours—
Sweeter thy breath than the odor of flowers—
Only thy smile can my sombre life brighten;
Come to me, darling, my sad heart to lighten.

You, when life's bitterness caused me to languish,
Rose like a star on the night of my anguish;

Nothing in life like thy dear presence blesses;
Come to me, darling, and meet my caresses.

Come joy or sorrow, I'll part from thee never—
Close to my bosom I'll press thee forever—
My heart is love's fountain laid open before thee;
Come to me, darling, and let it flow o'er thee.

THE DRUNKARD.

Hopelessly wandering through the cold street,
His clothes all in tatters, no shoes on his feet;
With countenance bloated, and rum-frenzied eye,
Tired of living, yet fearing to die,
How the crowd jeers as he shuffles along,
No look of pity or love in the throng;
How his heart burns as he looks on the scene,
Thinking of what *is* and what might have been!

Once he was youthful, light-hearted, and gay—
Life to him then seemed a long summer's day;
Now he is penniless, friendless, and old,
And shakes like a reed in the pitiless cold.
Once he had energy, freedom from fear,
A bright beaming eye, and an intellect clear;

'Twas seldom that sorrow or trouble would come,
Till he gave himself up to the demon of rum.

Drink was the serpent that wrought his first pain,
And fixed on his record unsullied, a stain;
Drink that he hailed as a friend in his glee,
But oh! what a fiend did that friend prove to be!
Slowly, but surely, with devilish art,
It palsied his strong frame and ate out his heart,
And placed the dark brand of disgrace on his brow,
And made him that wreck of a man he is now.

O ye who are under the rum-demon's spell,
And pour down your throats his vile poison of hell!

Of his subtle arts I beseech you beware,
Ere you find yourselves wrecked on the shoal of despair.
Ye may fight him awhile, but believe me, at length
The strongest will fall and succumb to his strength;
If you court him at all, you will struggle in vain
To break the strong links of the rum-demon's chain.

A CHRISTMAS STORY.

'Twas winter, and the frost king's breath
   Made piercing cold the air,
And the rude north wind, fierce and strong,
   Rushed through the forest bare,
Till e'en the gaunt and hungry wolf
   Sought shelter in his lair.

Near the highway, and just within
   The margin of a wood,
Lonely and drear, and frail with age,
   A time-worn hovel stood;
And there a wretched couple dwelt—
   Old John and Rachel Hood.

The keen blast whistled through the chinks,
   And shook the crazy door,

And pierced the aged pair as they
  The embers shivered o'er,
And groaned in bitterness of soul,
  To hear the tempest roar.

At length the old man with a sigh
  Upraised his hoary head,
And looking at the wrinkled dame,
  In savage humor said,
"O wife! I wish with all my soul
  That you and I were dead.

"This is a pretty Christmas day,
  Old dame, for you and I;
All gloom, and poverty, and rags,
  And abject misery!
'Twere better we were in our graves
  And sleeping tranquilly.

"The pampered rich are feasting now
  'Mid revelry and mirth,

And singing pretty madrigals
    About the Saviour's birth.
Curse 'em! I wish the Holy Babe
    Had never come on earth.

"How has His coming aided us?
    What favor have we met?
Our only son a wanderer,
    If he be living yet;
While we are old and poor, and **scarce**
    A crust of bread can get.

"Religion is a humbug, dame;
    'Tis only for the few
Who roll about in carriages,
    And not for me and you.
I'd sell myself to Satan,
    If he'd find me work to do!

"Hark! Listen, Rachel! What was that?
    I heard it once before!

It sounds like some one knocking
    For admittance at the door.
I heard it very plainly then,
    Above the tempest's roar!"

The wrinkled dame rose from her seat
    And opened wide the door,
And standing there, well wrapped in furs,
    A traveler they saw,
Whose face was bronzed, and who had lived
    Of years perhaps two score.

"A merry Christmas, friends!" he cried,
    As he surveyed the pair,
And then he wiped the frozen sleet
    From off his beard and hair,
And then he took a seat upon
    A rickety old chair.

The stranger looked the cabin o'er,
    And then continued he,

"But you're *not* over merry here,
    To judge from what I see;
There are few bosoms that rejoice
    When pinched by poverty.

"But cheer up, friends; I have the means
    To make your old hearts light,
And I will pay you well for food
    And shelter for the night.
I'll make you sing to-morrow morn
    If you but use me right."

And then the stranger merrily
    From his great pocket took
A purse of gold, and holding it
    Aloft, the metal shook;
The while the aged couple stared
    With desp'rate, greedy look.

Uprose the old man quickly then,
    And eagerly he said,

"We've little food to offer you
    And but a sorry bed;
But what we have is freely yours,
    Though we should go unfed."

"Enough, enough!" the stranger cried.
    "If you give all your store,
You do the very best you can—
    The best could do no more—
So set before me what you have,
    And compliments give o'er."

The meal dispatched, the traveler spoke:
    "Remember what I've said,
You'll merry be to-morrow morn,
    Unless I'm with the dead;
And so a kind good-night, old friends;
    Come, show me to my bed!"

An hour passed on—the stranger slept—
    And to the aged pair

It seemed as though a thousand fiends
    Were shrieking in the air,
As they with greedy, savage eyes
    Did at each other stare.

At length the old man stealthily
    His trembling wife drew near,
And while his white hair rose on end,
    He whispered in her ear;
And then a groan escaped her,
    And she shook with guilty fear.

"Why should we hesitate," he said,
    "To strike the fatal blow?
No soul on earth except ourselves
    The truth will ever know;
I'll do it, though the deed should plunge
    My soul in endless woe!"

Then crawling to the stranger's couch
    He raised on high a knife,

And struck the blow which took away
   The hapless victim's life—
Then clutched the gold and bore it to
   His half-demented wife.

*   *   *   *   *

The wretched pair sat cowering there
   Till rose the morning sun;
They could not sleep, for only half
   Their dreadful task was done,
And they dared not by candle-light
   Their victim look upon.

But now when rosy morning
   Had banished storm and night,
They raised the floor and sought the corpse
   To put it out of sight;
But, oh! their guilty souls were filled
   With horror and affright.

With shaking limbs they raised the dead,
   When suddenly the hair

Fell from the temples, and the dame
    With fixed and stony glare
Gazed on a curious mark, and screamed,
    "Look there, old man, look there!"

Transfixed they stood in speechless awe,
    And motion had they none,
And freezingly through all their veins
    Did their weak life-tide run;
"Great God!" shrieked out the murderer,
"We've killed our only son!"

    *   *   *   *   *   *

Oh! ye who scoff at God's decrees
    In unrepentant mood,
And sacrilegiously ignore
    A Saviour's precious blood,
Think of the fate which fell upon
    The dame and old John Hood.

S
.7

www.ingramcontent.com/pod-product-compliance
Lightning Source LLC
Chambersburg PA
CBHW032117230426
43672CB00009B/1769